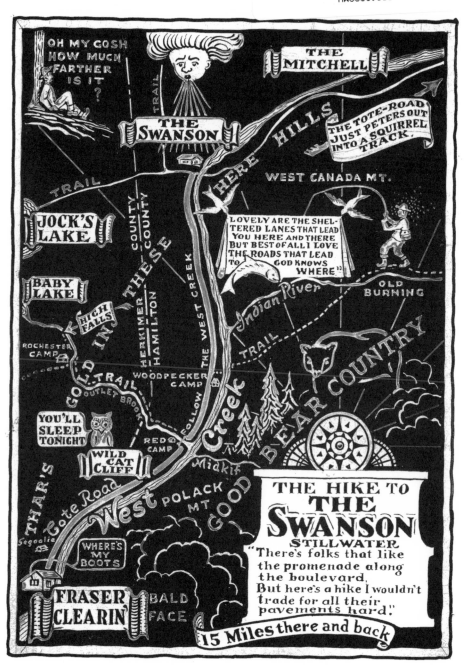

Illustrations by Harvey L. Dunham

Adirondack Adventures

Bob Gillespie & Harvey Dunham on French Louie's Trail

By Roy E. Reehil & William J. O'Hern
Introduction by Neal Burdick

🕊 The Forager Press, LLC

The Forager Press, LLC
23 Bridge St. Cleveland, New York 13042

Designed and illustrated by Roy E. Reehil
with illustrations from Harvey L. Dunham and Frank Devecis
Edited by Neal Burdick, Roy E. Reehil and Mary L. Thomas
Manufactured in the United States of America

Library of Congress Control Number: 2007926157
Publisher's Cataloging-in-Publication Data
Reehil, Roy E., 1957–
    Adirondack Adventures: Bob Gillespie and Harvey Dunham on French Louie's
Trail / by Roy E. Reehil and William J. O'Hern. — 1st ed.
        p. cm.
    Includes bibliographical references (p. 260) and index (p. 271).
    1. Gillespie, Robert (1877–1935)—Biography—Anecdotes.
2. Dunham, Harvey Leslie (1887–1956)—Biography—Anecdotes. 3. Seymour, Louis
(1832–1915)—Biography—Anecdotes. 4. Adirondack Mountains—Biography—Social
life and customs. 4. New York (State)—Adirondack Mountains—Social life and
customs. I. Reehil, Roy E., 1957– . II. Title.
F127.A2035 2012
974.75'53-dc25

Hard cover: ISBN-978-0-9743943-2-9
Paperback: ISBN-978-0-9743943-3-6

Cover and Jacket photographs courtesy of
Carolyn Browne Malkin & Robert C. Browne,
Edward Blankman (from the Lloyd Blankman Collection)
and Richard and Kathleen White.
Credits for the photographs and illustrations within the book
are located in the list of illustrations beginning on page 264.

The Forager Press, LLC is online at
www.TheForagerPress.com

To Robert Gillespie
and his family.

Contents

Preface

Saturday, August 16, 1919.

Ray Dunham, Jess Seitz and Bob Gillespie started from Syracuse at 3 P.M. on New York Central Local – (no first-class train would carry them) – arrived in Utica at 5 P.M. Harve Dunham left Albany at 12:55; arrived in Utica at 3:30. The whole bunch met in front of Bell Telephone Office at 11:15 P.M.. Got the tent and some other traps out of the office and took them down to New York Central Station at 12 midnight

Sunday, August 17th.

After a little lunch and witnessing a near scrap between a Canadian and a Jew, took the bunch of duffel and got on the 2:15 A.M. train at 2:10. Train finally pulled out at 2:40. arrived at Fulton Chain at 4:45, when we run into a rain storm. Harve butted into a bunch of girls and bummed a handout from one named Dot Knapp. They were going to 7th Lake and got off at Carter. Finally arrived at Beaver River at just daylight and at 5:30. It was a dark morning, but it had not rained there at all. The four of us explored about and inspected the whole place until 6:30 when Pop Bullock opened up his hotel, including the Post Office. We ordered breakfast for four, which was prepared by Deliah, and was ready a little after 7 o'clock. We also dug up Lee Beach, who runs the wagon to the river, and at 8:45 loaded the stuff on, including the eats which were at the station, and got down to the river at 9 o'clock. We found the canoe at the river. Also, we met Burt Darrow there who was on his way to Burnt Lake with a party

Grassy Point – Start of the trip Aug 17 1919.

A sample page from the journal that starts on page 70.

FROM THE FIRST GLIMPSES WE KNEW that the photo-journals that Carolyn Malkin had safeguarded for decades were remarkable. Her grandfather, Bob Gillespie, had assembled them to document fishing and camping trips he had made with friends and family to the Adirondacks between 1908 and 1924. The photographs of overflowing creels, scenic landscapes, and men decked out in tall boots, pack baskets and fedoras were alone fantastic, but on closer inspection, the text that accompanied the photographs revealed a depth of observation and humor that was truly unique. We'd seen diaries and photo albums before, but none that so perfectly expressed the partnership of men in the wilderness with such vivid style.

Magnifying our curiosity was that one of the writers of the collaborative text was none other than Harvey L. Dunham, the author of the book *Adirondack French Louie—Early Life in the North Woods.* The significance of Dunham's appearance in the journals was that we both credited his classic collection of Adirondack folklore as "the book" that had started us down different paths that ended in the same place—where we both became amateur historians and authors.

We'd both read *"French Louie"* several times. We'd both visited some of Louie's campsites and haunts. We'd both dug deeper into the history of the region on our own, but of Dunham himself, we knew almost nothing. He died in 1956, four years after self-publishing the book, and melted away in relative obscurity. But there he was, alongside Carolyn's grandfather having the time of their lives. The feeling we shared at Carolyn's dining room table as we thumbed though the fragile old journals was not so different from that of wide-eyed children on Christmas morning. Our curiosity was piqued. What light would the journals shed on Dunham's past? Who was Bob Gillespie and what was his connection to Dunham? Did Bob and the trips he and Harvey made together have a connection to the writing of Dunham's inspiring book?

It didn't take long for us to conclude that the journals were worthy of publication, but we also realized that if we could discover the answers to our questions about Bob Gillespie and Harvey Dunham we might have a bigger story—one that might lead all the way to French Louie. Now we can show you what we found.

We appreciate the privilege afforded to us by Carolyn Browne Malkin and her brother, Robert C. Browne, for sharing their grandfather's accounts. With the greatest respect for the men who created the journals, we present their stories.

—Roy E. Reehil & William J. O'Hern

Authors' Note

Though at first we thought we might be able to reproduce the Gillespie journals exactly as they were, it was quickly decided that there were too many technical difficulties to do so. Instead, we transcribed the journals as they were written and left in all but the worst grammatical errors and potentially offensive language.

We offer this note in advance of the journal entries, old newspaper articles and quoted material, that they are all presented *sic erat scriptum*—"thus was it written." We have added occasional words for clarity and footnotes to explain unusual terms or phrases, but for the most part all of the dated material has been left as it was written.

Bob's marked-up topographical maps could also not be reproduced, so we created a set of illustrated maps that, though not perfectly to scale, do indicate the basic "lay of the land." True aficionados of map and compass use or "bushwhacking" may want to have a set of topographical maps handy while reading, to increase your perspective of the terrain and distances the men surmounted and to enhance your reading experience.

Introduction

By Neal Burdick

P EOPLE JUST DON'T TAKE VACATIONS LIKE THEY USED TO.
Some vacations were a lot more work in the "good old days." No
lounging around and being waited on at poolside back then;
the "strenuous life" championed by Teddy Roosevelt was the goal, at
least among a certain segment of the populace.

Consider the Adirondack summer outings undertaken by Bob
Gillespie, Harvey Dunham and an assortment of friends a century or
so ago: Climb onto a train in the wee hours of the night; get off at a
remote depot in the Adirondack forests before sunup; undergo a long,
bumpy wagon ride and then a hike of several miles, hauling fishing
and camping gear and many pounds of foodstuffs (this was before
the days of freeze-dried dinners and gorp, remember; we're talking
canned goods and sacks of flour); get bewildered on an old logging
road; make a raft to get across a pond; repeat at the next pond; set up
camp; catch trout for dinner. Do much the same every day for two
weeks; then slog out.

All this regardless of the weather. And oh, did it rain! Reading the
camping journals of Dunham, Gillespie and their companions, they may
as well have built an ark as a series of rafts, for all the deluges they got
caught in. If their reports are accurate, the Adirondacks of the World
War I years were definitely not suffering from drought conditions.

You won't find scrapbooks of vacations like these anymore, either.
The trip accounts were neat as a pin, with hardly a typo in sight. A gen-
erous supply of snapshots are squared up and affixed with old-fashioned
black corner tabs that you can find in aging family photo albums. First
names or initials at the end of each section indicate the party member
responsible for the report.

All of the entries are well-crafted, but one thing becomes clear in reading Dunham's contributions: the man could write. His accounts of adventures in the backwoods of the southern Adirondacks are entertaining, literate, highly readable and grammatically nearly flawless, allowing for a few idiosyncrasies of the times that we don't see today. So it's no wonder he eventually wrote a book about "Adirondack French Louie" Seymour, certified character and legendary denizen of the region Dunham and his compatriots frequented. It could be said that his journal-writing was a long-term warm-up for his classic book, in which the otherwise pedestrian office-worker saw his writing penchant, honed in his outing journals, blossom into full flower.

All of this Roy Reehil and Jay O'Hern lay out in this volume whose hub is Dunham's writing but that swings jauntily out into ancillary territory, always circling back to Dunham. Part I, about the men, the places they travelled and their journals, gives us lively accounts of fishing expeditions into the backcountry; Part II introduces us to French Louie and how Dunham gathered anecdotes and wrote his noteworthy volume about him.

Always hovering in the background, sometimes exploding into the forefront, is the story of the State of New York's conflicted attitude toward the wild country and its inhabitants, whether they be William Seward Webb, who wouldn't let a mere state law stop him from building a railroad wherever he wanted to, or the rich power-brokers of the Adirondack League Club, or nettlesome, fiercely independent loners like French Louie, who would rather converse with his pet snakes than with any politician or puffed-up millionaire. Or just plain folks, like Dunham, his mentor Gillespie and supporting cast members who come and go across this stage, like the Rev. A. L. Byron-Curtiss, who simply wanted a little place in the woods where he could go to get away from the trials of civilization. The story of French Louie's chimney and its frequent brushes with demolition at the hands of by-the-book bureaucrats, and finally its salvation as an almost accidental historic landmark, is a parallel thread that helps bring this tale to its conclusion.

Simultaneously, we have between these covers an undercurrent that portrays the evolution of the southern Adirondack region as it stumbled out of the heyday of lumbering and made its first tentative forays into the era of mass tourism. The region was in the midst of a long-term reinvention of itself from one in which the main economic material, wood, went out, into one in which the main economic material, people, came in. The gentlemen who wrote the journals featured here were among many who were the vanguard of that movement over a period of years. That they occasionally came upon relics of the halcyon logging days as they went about the serious business of finding the best fishing holes is symbolic of the shift.

We also learn much about Gillespie, Dunham, their families and their close associates, not only from the journals but also from the background that Reehil and O'Hern fill in the cracks with. These were real people, after all, not just journal-scribbling fishermen; they had jobs and wives and kids and successes and tragedies, just like all of us. Through this work, we are privileged to come to know a little bit about them.

And then there was French Louie, to whom we are given a good, solid introduction, the better to know "da man" Dunham wrote about. They don't make the likes of him anymore; it's doubtful whether, in this day and age, anyone would be able, or allowed, to live the way he did, a happy vagrant squatting on land of uncertain ownership and visiting civilization (for him the metropolis of Speculator) once or twice a year to gather up what little human contact he needed, and to cut loose, just because he could. This tantalizing glimpse of a unique citizen will make you want to track down Dunham's biography and read it.

Before you do, though, it's important that you read the rest of this book. Once you've done that, you'll have the right context, the right frame of mind, for both fishing and further reading. For through this book you will understand a lot more about the back woods of the southern Adirondacks: the lay of the land, some of the myriad unique individuals who loved them, and the political currents that ebbed and flowed upon their shores in days gone by.

Part I

The Adirondack Adventures of Harvey Dunham & Bob Gillespie

Harvey Dunham and Bob Gillespie

Chapter 1
Friends for Life

TROUT POND

SUNLIGHT SPLASHED across the surface of Trout Pond, where a lone fisherman's jonboat bobbed with the breeze. The fisherman's attention was fixed upon his rod tip until some rustling onshore caught his ear. He looked up and watched as a wobbly, inverted canoe emerged from the wall of forest, perched above a torso with two skinny legs. The legs were attached to Harvey Dunham, who would one day write the renowned book of regional folklore called *Adirondack French Louie—Early Life in the North Woods.*

Dunham recalled his meeting with the fisherman in verse:

I met him in the mountains
Up Beaver River way,
He was fishing on Trout Pond
On a sunny August day.

He said "My name's Gillespie,
I know your brother Ray."
I said "I'm glad to know you."
(I'll say the same today.)

I shoved the canoe across the pond,
Gillespie docked his boat.
"I'll give you a hand on the trail," says he,
And started in to tote.

His lift was what I needed
To make the camp that night.
The pack he carried on that trail,
You couldn't call it light.

And so we packed together
From Salmon to West Crick,
And as we pack on through the years,
I never hear Bob kick.

The two of them did carry Harvey Dunham's canoe to Salmon Lake that day, less than a mile up the tote road from Trout Pond, but Dunham's reference to packing together "From Salmon to West Crick" was not literal. West Crick, or rightly West Canada Creek, is where Harvey Dunham and Bob Gillespie eventually owned property together and built several camps. By the time Harvey wrote his poem, "West

Ray Dunham

Crick" had come to symbolize the lifelong friendship that he and Bob began that day—"up Beaver River way."

Bob had camped at Salmon Lake with Harvey's older brother Ray before, so there was plenty to talk about during their first canoe carry. At the southern tip of Salmon Lake, they loaded into Harvey's canoe and paddled to "Camp Happy," Elmer Wilder's place at the northwest end of the lake.

In the days before the state deterred people from taking up residence on state land, Elmer built a cabin for his wife and three daughters on a tranquil bay with a little room left over for guests. Once Bob discovered Camp Happy, he, along with friends and family, became frequent patrons.

In preceding years Bob had fished for brook trout in many of the waters within bushwhacking distance of the train

Elmer Wilder

stations along the Adirondack Division of the New York Central & Hudson River Railroad, but the Beaver River region became his favorite destination and Camp Happy his favorite base camp. Surrounded by almost unlimited wilderness and acres of ponds, rivers and lakes, the area was ripe for exploring, one of Bob's preferred pastimes.

Bob was also interested in home photography so, when those interests converged, the result was an illustrated travel log, a journal that he began assembling in 1912. With a mechanical typewriter and a wax pencil, Bob captioned his hazy, imperfect photographs—probably developed in a bathroom or basement darkroom—and carefully pasted them down on the black pages of a leather-covered album. Along with his photographs he added postcards, newspaper clippings and topographical maps marked with important landmarks. His captions identified most of the people and places, and the longer typed passages completed the story of his early Adirondack explorations.

As Bob's meticulous journal-making evolved, two more albums followed, but they were different from the first. Rather than combining the records of many trips from different years into one album, each of the later journals chronicled a single two-week camping trip, one in 1919 and one in 1924. For these, Bob brought along notebooks and made it clear to his camping buddies that they were welcome (or perhaps duty-bound) to write about their observations and activities. The men responded with good-humored writing, the kind that told their story but also contained plenty of lightly-camouflaged humor.

Upon his return, Bob typed up the contents of the field notes and processed his black and white film into appropriately sized prints. He then assembled the pieces into lengthy leather-bound books.

The resulting documents are not only descriptive of the remote places that the men visited, but are filled with the honesty and ribbing you might expect among good friends, all written in the colloquialisms of the 1920s.

Although Bob probably created the journals for no other reason than to share memories and laughs with his friends and family, today they provide a rare and personal glimpse back to a time when long-distance travel was best accomplished by train; when canvas, cotton, silk and wool were the preferred fabrics for camping; and when backpacks were woven baskets, with leather, cotton or canvas straps.

We hope the men would be pleased that we are enjoying their stories today, particularly Bob, who wrote this eloquent preface to his first journal:

This book is the property of Bob Gillespie. The pictures herein were made mostly by myself or friends. In the making of this book, I have had much pleasure. Every picture means something to me. If my friends are interested in this book, I am glad of it. If they are fortunate enough to be able to go to the woods, I would like to have them go to the same places that I have been and then we will have something in common. I know of no better way to spend a vacation than to go up to God's country.

For an outdoorsman, his preface is an invitation. Go there; explore! There is "no better way to spend a vacation."

Chapter 2
Bob Gillespie and Beaver River Country

Brothers Zene and Bob Gillespie

ROBERT MARCUS or "Bob" Gillespie was born on June 9, 1877, in Providence, Pennsylvania. His friends described him as "smart, amiable and fun to be around." His writings certainly reinforce that sentiment. He grew up in Dunmore and Scranton, Pennsylvania, with his parents and two brothers, Zenus, who was known as "Zene," and Jared. His mother died when the boys were young, and a housekeeper raised them for a number of years until Bob's father married Frances Palmer from Erie. They later moved to Elmira, New York, where Bob and Zene graduated from Elmira Free Academy.

"The boys were forever swept away with playing outdoors," reported Bob's granddaughter Carolyn Malkin, relaying some family history that had been passed down to her. "My grandmother gave away some of her husband's youthful secrets after he died."

As Carolyn told one story, "The Gillespie boys were never youngsters that could sit through an entire Sunday church service." They would "steal out of church to slip dynamite from the tool shed," so it was not uncommon to hear an explosion from somewhere beyond their church hall. Parishioners tried to focus on the service, but it was hard not to notice the poorly-concealed smiles on the faces that betrayed what the Gillespie boys were up to.

She also related a sadder story. "Jared raced motorcycles and was in an accident during a race. The doctor assured the family that he didn't need a tetanus shot after the accident, but he died of tetanus because he didn't receive the shot. My mother and her sister were old enough to remember that, and the family never got over that."

She added that "Zene lived his adult life somewhere in New England and owned a hardware store there named Gillespie Hardware. I wish I knew where. I have a small paring knife at camp that came from that store."

As a youth, Bob nurtured his sporting nature in the Southern Tier of New York, but the reports he heard while growing up of abundant fish and wildlife in the Adirondacks were a strong lure. One of the places that caught Bob's attention was the Beaver River region in the Western Adirondacks because it "had it all": long stretches of wild river; trout ponds by the dozen connected by carrying trails; hotels with guides for hire; and railroads being built to make it all more accessible.

In an 1889 edition of his *Descriptive Guide to the Adirondacks,* Edwin R. Wallace provided an example of what Bob may have read about the Beaver River region before he decided to travel there.

Beaver River (Indian, Ne-ha-sa-ne, "crossing on a log") is 80 or 90 miles long, and from its extreme source, within 100 rods of Beach's Lake (Trout Pond), and within 5 or 6 miles of Raquette Lake, flows in a southwesterly direction, in a line nearly parallel with that of Moose River, draining in its passage 70 or 80 handsome lakes and ponds, and discharging its waters into the Black River, some 8 miles

Stillwater Reservoir on the Beaver River.

below Lowville, near Castorland. Fifty miles of its course is buried in a dense, unbroken wilderness, rarely trodden by the foot of man, and but 3 or 4 habitations . . . indicate any encroachment upon its primitive character. Throughout most of this distance, the scenery investing its borders is full of wildness, sometimes of beauty.

. . . Two miles above that, a stream empties into the Beaver, flowing from a series of 12 or 15 lakes and ponds, termed the "Red Horse Chain,"[1] which furnish very attractive scenery, and are regarded as superior fishing and hunting localities. They are accessible with boats over passable portages. . . .

From near the head of Salmon Lake (little white birches marking the spot) a carry leads northwest over a mountain 1-¾ miles to Hawk, or Emerald Lake. This is so imprisoned within a circle of forest-clad mountains, as to form a charming picture.

The guidebook descriptions were enticing, but probably not the only way that the Beaver River and the Red Horse Chain entered Bob's imagination. During the early 1890s, controversy over plans for the region, which would in effect divide, develop and tame the last stretches of wilderness there, put the Adirondacks into newspaper headlines across the state.

[1] Named for the red horse sucker abounding in an inlet of one of these lakes.

Chapter 3
The Forest
Becomes a Park

Wherever the railroads go the forests disappear.
—Forest Commissioner Sherman Knevals, May 1891

B OB GILLESPIE WAS A TEENAGER as the debate over the future
of the Adirondack forest came to a head. "The Big Forest in
Danger," "Railroad Schemes to Ruin the State Preserve," and
"The Passing Away of the Forests" were some of the grim headlines that
Bob may have encountered. No matter what he thought about those
headlines at the time, the outcome of the controversy would affect the
places he would be able to visit and what he would see when he got
there. Would he find "Mile after Mile of the Old Woods Converted
into a Waste of Stumps and Stones" or "The People's Park in the
Adirondacks," as two competing *New York Times* headlines predicted?
The latter article described the encroachment of the industries capable
of denuding the forest this way:

> The lumber and tanning companies are penetrating with their
> railways every portion of this great wilderness. . . . In another year
> magnificent trees, as old as the Republic, grand old groves [of]
> shrubbery, will have disappeared before the lumberman, the tanner,
> and the charcoal burner, and cannot for centuries be restored. Still
> further, private clubs and associations of sportsmen are getting pos-
> session of the best sporting grounds and the most attractive lakes,
> and though they may protect the forest they will close some of the
> loveliest resorts to the public.

Just as the debate was gaining steam, Dr. William Seward Webb, who had married into the Vanderbilt family of railroad tycoons, had quietly accumulated nearly a quarter million acres of mostly pristine Adirondack land with two objectives in mind: to section off the largest private park in the Adirondacks and to build a railroad that would connect the Mohawk Valley to Montreal, bisecting the center of the Adirondack wilderness. At the time,

Dr. William Seward Webb

few people had any idea what Dr. Webb had in mind, but that was all about to change. A convergence of events was beginning that would help determine the future of the entire mountain region.

The Adirondack Park did not yet exist, so the legislation that had passed in 1885 creating the Forest Preserve protected only land that the state already owned—and that was only about 700,000 acres that had been heavily logged and abandoned to the state for non-payment of taxes. Though there had been talk of creating an "Adirondack Park" ever since Verplanck Colvin, Superintendent of the Adirondack Survey, had first voiced his opinion that the whole Adirondack region "should be set aside . . . as a park . . . as is the Yosemite for California" in an 1870 report, it wasn't until the 1890s that the public paid enough attention to agitate the State Legislature to action.

In June of 1890, the Adirondack League Club was formed and by August it had purchased 104,000 acres of nearly contiguous virgin timber, one of the few stands of its kind left in the Adirondacks. Their goal was to create a gigantic private preserve, ringed with posted signs. This idea was an affront to nearby residents, many of whom had earned a living or helped provide food for their families by hunting, fishing, foraging or trapping in the region for a generation or more. In a further

Logging near Stillwater on the Beaver River.

incitement of the locals, the club installed a screen at the outlet of
Honnedaga Lake [formerly Jocks Lake] to block their well-renowned
"fat trout" from escaping back onto publicly accessed waterways. This
threatened "locking out" of the public and "locking in" of nature played
into the hands of preservationists and stirred public anger.

To counter the expansion of private clubs, a group of New York City
physicians formed a group called the Adirondack Park Association,[2]
dedicated to "the preservation of the Adirondack forests . . . and . . .
the establishment of a state forest park."

Newspaper columnists latched onto the preservationist bandwagon
and attacked the lumber companies and railroads as forces of destruction. Congress had protected both Yosemite and Sequoia by designating
them as National Parks in the fall of 1890; why couldn't the same thing
be done to protect the great forests in New York?

Momentum was building to establish such a park in the Adirondacks,
when the Forest Commission sent a proposal to the State Legislature.

---

[2] In order not to be confused with the current Adirondack Park Association, the name of the
association was changed to the Adirondack North Country Association in 1983. In May 1891, the
association was accused of either being turn-coats or of "organizing under false pretenses" when
they switched their position to one of support for Webb's railroad after being assured by Webb
that "...as a land owner he was deeply interested in protecting [the forest] from destruction...."

The proposal consisted of a map with a blue line drawn on it delineating the borders of an "Adirondack Park," and a bill providing the state with the ability to acquire land to add to the Forest Preserve. The bill also proposed to make it illegal to sell or exchange Forest Preserve land without the consent of the Forest Commission.

The "sell or exchange" provisions quickly drew the attention of Dr. Webb because, if the bill passed, he would lose the ability to acquire the last strips of land that he needed to complete his railroad through the Adirondacks. Sensing that the State Legislature would be slow to act, Webb sprang into action. By February of 1891, he had purchased existing railroad companies at either end of his proposed line. The Herkimer, New York and Poland was a narrow-gauge line that Webb would widen, and the Mohawk and St. Lawrence was a potential competitor that also had planned to lay rails through the Adirondacks to Malone.

Then on April 1, Dr. Webb sent a telegram to a leading citizen of Malone saying that he would arrive the next day to arrange for construction of his railroad. The telegram was at first considered an April Fool's joke, but Webb arrived and called a meeting of townspeople to offer them a proposition: "Raise $30,000, secure its payment to me when the [rail]road is finished and in operation, and I will build a railroad from your village through the Adirondacks to Herkimer or Schenectady, skirting the Saranacs, the first fifty miles to be completed in four months and the entire line in two years."

Webb didn't wait for an answer. His surveyors were afield days later and, not surprisingly, the bond was secured within days after that. Not every New Yorker was against building the railroad, least of all in Malone, but now that Webb's plans were known a race was on to build the railroad faster than his opposition could move to stop him.

His next move shrewdly pitted the jurisdiction of one state office against another. Webb applied to the Land Office to purchase land within the Forest Preserve that he needed to complete the line. Again, he didn't wait for a resolution. He sent his surveyors to mark the line,

Main Street, Malone, N.Y.

anticipating success. When questions were raised about the legality of the purchase, Webb was prepared with a piece of property of greater value to offer in trade, a legal maneuver that the Land Office accepted and could not be overruled.

Soon, nearly four thousand men were laying rails from the northernmost and southernmost extents of the Adirondacks as fast as the land could be cleared and leveled. Cost was no object. Webb ordered that his line be built at a "spikes-per-mile" quality standard exceeding that of nearly every railroad in the country. The "Mohawk and Malone," as Webb had named it, soon became known as "Webb's Golden Chariot Route" due to the amazing flow of men, money and materials engaged in the project. "His money is flowing into woods like the brooks" wrote a *New York Herald* reporter.

To further speed construction, one enlightened subcontractor put a barrel of beer far ahead of the track layers with the promise that they could share it once the stretch was done. Not surprisingly, the work proceeded at a record pace. But happy workers or not, once Webb's railroad and private park plans were splashed in negative headlines across the state, a public outcry ignited. "Dr. Webb's Railroad Will Make a Desert of the Adirondacks" read one May 1891 headline in the *New York Times*. In June, the paper printed an article

attacking Webb's plans for a private preserve. The article's title was
"By Permission of Dr. Webb."

> Sportsmen...who for many years have made visits to the Adirondacks
> a part of their Summer outings are not very well pleased with the turn
> affairs have taken in that region. The recent purchase by Dr. Seward
> Webb of all the lands lying around the headwaters of the Beaver River
> excludes them from the best hunting and fishing grounds in the State
> and practically puts up the bars against all who are not able to pay a
> good round price for the privilege of enjoying that kind of sport.
>
> Dr. Webb's tract of 250,000 acres takes in Albany, Smith, Twitchell,
> Big Moose, Wood, Sylvan, Loon, Negro and Crooked Lakes,[3] besides
> all the lakes in the Red Horse chain and many small ponds that are
> famous for trout and deer. This tract is what Mr. Webb is pleased to
> call Ne-ha-sa-ne Park.... His domain, when fully secured, will meet
> the lands of the Adirondack League Club on the east.
>
> These two preserves take in all the good fishing and hunting
> grounds in Hamilton, Herkimer and Lewis Counties, and the whole
> tract is now closed to the public so far as shooting and fishing is
> concerned. The hotels and camps receive no guests, and a score
> or more of men in the employ of Dr. Webb are stationed in the
> woods to warn visitors to keep off the lakes and streams. A party of
> Watertown sportsmen who were ignorant of the new order of things
> in the Beaver River region went up there last week for a few days'
> fishing. They had scarcely made a cast before they were notified by
> Webb's men to quit, and their attention was called to notices that had
> been posted forbidding all persons to fish or hunt in that locality....
> They came out of the woods fully convinced that the day when the
> Adirondacks could be called the poor man's resort would not come
> again for a generation.

[3] The names of several of these lakes have been changed since this article was written. Dr. Webb renamed Smith Lake to Lake Lila for his wife, Lila Osgood Vanderbilt Webb, the daughter of William H. Vanderbilt. He also renamed Albany Lake to Nehasane Lake. Negro Lake was called by the more offensive "N-word" until it was changed in 1965. Throughout the rest of this book we refer to it as Negro Lake.

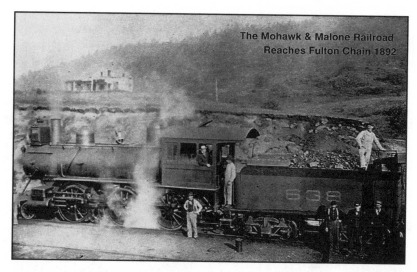

The Mohawk & Malone Railroad
Reaches Fulton Chain 1892

These articles and others like them helped motivate the State Legislature. In May 1892, they passed the law that codified the "blue line" delineating the Adirondack State Park, and although they may have been encouraged to action by public opposition to Webb's railroad, in the end, the legislation was too late to stop it. All of the land swaps, tax-sale reversals and back room deals that were made to attain the last strips of Forest Preserve to complete the railroad were signed before the law took effect, and Webb's men were laying track before the ink was dry on the contracts.

By October 1892, it was clear. Webb had won. The last spike was driven to complete the railroad between Big Moose and the Beaver River. Trains would steam through the heart of the Adirondacks and the legislation that might have ended the endeavor ironically now protected Webb from new competition.

But the controversies surrounding the railroad and the impact it might have on the region were changing public perceptions. There was little argument that the railroad would lead to more rapid settlement and lumber harvesting. The bigger question was the extent to which the resulting deforestation would inhibit the forest that remained from providing an adequate flow of water to the great rivers of New York. If the claims of distinguished preservationists like Verplanck Colvin

Rounding the bend at milepost 68, about a mile south of Big Moose Station.

were even half true, the effects on drinking water supplies, the canal system and ultimately the economy of New York could be devastating. Hyperbole was rampant on both sides and increased the public's awareness of the dire predictions.

A few months later and contrary to public sentiment, Governor Flower signed a law that, instead of reducing the ability of the five-member Forest Commission to sell timber, dramatically increased it. The disappointing action caused Frank Gardner, Secretary of the New York Board of Trade and Transportation, to mutter, "I am convinced that the forests will never be made safe until they are put into the State Constitution." The comment proved to be the necessary inspiration to find a way to place the Forest Preserve beyond the reach of political tinkering.

The wait was short. The opportunity to act came in May 1894, when a State Constitutional Convention was convened for reasons entirely other than forest preservation. In fact, the majority Republicans had not even formed any committees to deal with forest issues at all. Regardless of that, a draft amendment was presented to the Hon. Joseph Choate, president of the convention. After reading the hastily drawn draft, Mr. Choate proclaimed, "You have brought here the most important question before this assembly. In fact, it is the only question that warrants the existence of this convention."

The Hon. David McClure, a Democrat, was allowed to present the amendment to the convention in what was said to be a "stirring speech." Shortly thereafter, the Republican majority called for a special committee to be formed, and appointed McClure to be its Chairman, an unusually bipartisan move that highlighted the importance of the measure in the eyes of convention delegates. The amendment, if ratified, would end the type of land exchanges that Dr. Webb employed to piece together his railroad and would outlaw all logging on Forest Preserve lands.

When the committee completed its debate and revisions, the remarkably sleek amendment read as follows:

"The lands of the State, now owned or fixed hereafter acquired, constituting the forest preserve as fixed by law, shall be forever kept as wild forest lands. They shall not be leased, sold, or exchanged, or be taken by any corporation, public or private, nor should the timber thereon be sold, removed, or destroyed."

On September 13, 1894, the convention delegates gathered to vote. The result was a resounding 122–0 approval—the first constitutional amendment so honored in state history. Now the question would be asked of the people. That hurdle was leapt on Election Day 1894, when by a fifty-six to forty-four percent margin, the iconic language that has since become known as the "Forever Wild Amendment" became part of the New York State Constitution.

But, what about the Red Horse Chain? "Forever wild" had finally passed, but it pertained only to state land. Dr. Webb still owned the Red Horse Chain with designs to log it and seal it off as part of his private preserve. The fate of the region twisted again as the level of the Beaver River rose.

By 1894, nearly every lake and river in Northern New York had been tapped to increase the flow of commerce-sustaining waters to the Black River and Erie Canals. Lakes Woodhull, South, North, Wolf, Kayuta, Sand, Twin, Canachagala, White, the Bisbys, and several lakes in the Fulton Chain were tapped, as well as the Black, Moose, Beaver, Independence and Mohawk Rivers—a mammoth impoundment system restraining some four billion cubic feet of water. As part of that system, the state's Superintendent of Public Works had been authorized to build a new dam, five feet higher than the previous one at Stillwater on the Beaver River.

By another coincidence, the dam at Stillwater was also finished in 1894. It wasn't planned to be completed in time for passage of the "Forever Wild Amendment" to change how lawsuits over flooding would be resolved, or to stop the harvest of virgin timber from the Red Horse Chain. It just happened that way. In the normal course of government affairs, appropriations were made, plans were drawn, contracts were bid and the work commenced. When the dam was completed and everything was made ready, the sluice gates were closed and the Beaver River swelled. And it swelled and it swelled to Mississippi River-like proportions, widening from a previous average of fifty feet across to a new average of 1,100 feet.

When the flooding ceased it had pushed upstream over 20 miles and flooded some 21,000 acres. Shortly thereafter, Dr. Webb sued the state, claiming that 13,000 of the flooded acres were his and that it was no longer feasible for him to log the valuable virgin timber north of the Beaver River.

It took two years of offers, studies and legal wrangling to settle the suit. In the end, a report by the State Forest, Game and Fisheries Commission concluded that it was ". . . satisfied with the justice of Mr. Webb's Claim." Under the agreement, Webb received $600,000 for land and "damages"—substantially more than the going rate per acre at the time—but the state acquired the 75,377 acres encompassing the Red Horse Chain. The "Webb Purchase," as it became known, held

The well-preserved remains of one of the earlier dams at Stillwater were exposed when the reservoir was lowered in 1925 to build a new dam.

the record as the largest parcel added to the Forest Preserve for over a century. Rather than being logged off and closed to the public, the area is today one of the few places in the Northeast United States where anyone with the gumption to do it can hike through or camp in a virgin aboriginal forest.

It's hard to say what Bob Gillespie and Harvey Dunham thought about Dr. Webb, but Bob did scribble a caption under a map of the newly raised Stillwater Reservoir in one of his journals that sums up his opinion of the management of the Beaver River: "New flow line after the pirates get through with the work of destruction."

It should be mentioned that, however vilified Dr. Webb was in some quarters, he was also widely celebrated for his achievements and in many circles was quite beloved. He adopted the most scientific and sustainable logging practices known at the time, and wrote a covenant that prevented the use or sale of all the land he would sell in the Adirondacks for "commercial-agricultural" or "manufacturing" purposes.

Left: The hamlet of Fulton Chain (now Thendara.) Center: Waiting for the train at Fulton Chain.

An excursion steamer on First Lake at Old Forge.

In 1896, the town of Wilmurt was divided so that the northern portion could be renamed the Town of Webb in his honor. Webb's railroad brought prosperity to many communities and, for better or worse, opened the Adirondack region to the tourism boom that was to come. One such tourist was a young "sport" from Elmira named Bob Gillespie.

Chapter 4

Bob's First Trip
to Beaver River

Beaver River Station.

WHATEVER BOB THOUGHT ABOUT the Mohawk and Malone railroad, he was inclined to use it, travelling by train to Beaver River for the first time in 1895, the year he turned eighteen. What an adventure it must have been, travelling from Elmira to the Adirondacks in the heyday of the steam powered locomotive, his fishing pole, pack basket and a heart filled with anticipation along for the ride.

As he peered out the window, station after station passed by, bustling with enterprise and surrounded with the signs of growth and industry. Wherever a station had been built, settlers, businessmen and laborers had followed, energizing the economies of the towns and hamlets along the new railroad corridor.

Smoke and steam billowed from the locomotive as the winding ascent out of the Mohawk Valley began. It would take a fully stoked engine to attain the full elevation of the southern Adirondacks. Higher and higher they climbed and one by one, the station's names were called out—Remsen; Honnedaga; Forestport; White Lake; Otter Lake; McKeever; Minnehaha; Fulton Chain; Big Moose; Woods Lake. Bob heard the "whooo-hoo" of the train whistle many times that day, but finally it indicated imminent arrival at his destination. "Next stop, Beaver River Station," the conductor shouted.

Bob later described Beaver River Station and the "Red Horse Chain" in 1913. A facsimile of the map he refers to appears on page 74.

Beaver River Station is on the Mohawk & Malone Division of the New York Central, seventy-two miles north of Utica. At the Station there are 200 acres of land owned by a man by the name of Monroe Bullock. Aside from the Railroad Station, there are no other buildings except the hotel and the barn. All of the rest of the land is owned by the State. The hotel is run by Bert Bullock, a son of Monroe Bullock.

The Hotel Norridgewock at Beaver River Station.
Bob later added that the hotel burned down in 1914.

Very good board can be had at this hotel for $2.00 a day, or from $9.00 to $12.00 per week. From the Station to the river, a distance of 1-¼ miles, is a very good wagon road. At the end of this road by the river is a little hotel run by Monroe Bullock. Board can be had here for $2.00 per day or $9.00 per week. Monroe Bullock or "Pop" Bullock, as he is always known, also has

"Pop" Bullock, the oldest resident of Beaver River, N.Y.

some boats here, and these can be used in getting across the river. On the north side of the river, as shown on the map [on page 74], there is a tote road. This road was originally used to tote supplies to some lumber camps off toward the northwest. The walking on this road is fine and it runs through Virgin Forest.

"Pop" Bullock on the porch of his inn at Grassy Point,
a mile and a quarter down the wagon road from Beaver River Station.

Top to bottom: The inlet to Salmon Lake, Camp Happy, Elmer Wilder, children playing at the outlet of Salmon Lake. Facing page: Salmon Lake viewed from the south shore.

Following this road for a distance of about 1-¼ miles, which takes just twenty-five minutes walking, you will come to where a trail crosses the road. This trail leads north for about ¾ of a mile along the outlet of Salmon Lake to the south end of the lake. Usually there is a boat or two on the lake which can be used to row to the north end of the lake to the camp of Elmer Wilder, as shown on the map. This camp is run by Elmer Wilder and his wife and three little girls. Board here can be had for $1.50 per day or $8.00 per week. The board is good and the beds are clean and the table linen is white.

Salmon Lake is one of the lakes in what is known as the Red Horse Chain. This chain of lakes takes its name from a small sucker fish which is known as the Red Horse Sucker. In the Spring of the year, the belly of this fish is a bright red. The first lake in the chain is Big Burnt, the second is Trout Pond, the third is Salmon Lake, the fourth is Witchhopple, the fifth is Mud Pond, the sixth is Clear Lake and the seventh is Summit Pond. To the north of Summit Pond is another watershed and another chain of lakes. Big Crooked Lake, as shown on the map, has the highest elevation in that chain of lakes.

On Witchhopple Lake, there is a camp, or rather a club, known as the Rap-Shaw Fishing Club. This camp is run by Jimmy Wilder, a cousin of Elmer Wilder. In order to put up at this camp, you have to be a member of the Club. Back of Elmer Wilder's camp on Salmon Lake is a first class trail leading to Hawk Pond. From Hawk Pond north is a first class trail to Willys Lake. There is no boat on Hawk Pond as there are no fish in this Pond. There are two or three boats on Willys Lake. From the northeast part of Willys Lake, there is a trail over to Walker Lake. Also, from the northeast part of Walker Lake, there is a trail down to the main trail between Witchhopple Lake and Mud Pond. There are boats on Clear and Big Crooked Lakes.

Above: The Rap-Shaw Fishing Club Camp on Witchopple Lake. Right: Jimmy Wilder, Elmer Wilder's cousin.

All these trails, as shown on the map, are cut out and kept free from brush, and are marked by blazes on the trees. All of this section of the woods is owned by the State and no trees have ever been cut. Anyone has a perfect right to camp where they please and no one can stop them. The permanent camps that are located in this section have been there for a number of years and, while the owners have no vested rights, the State permits them to live there during the summer months and these people protect the forests from fires and also do not permit the cutting of any standing timber. All of the lakes in this section, with the exception of Hawk Pond and Dismal Pond, have brook trout and lake trout in them and, as a general proposition, the fishing is first class.

—*Bob Gillespie*

Chapter 5
A Telephone Man

Ella Mae and Bob Gillespie on the dock at Camp Happy.

ON MARCH 1, 1897, Bob went to work as a "shophand" in Elmira for the New York and Pennsylvania Telephone and Telegraph Company. He was nineteen years old and remained a "telephone man" for the rest of his life. He became a splicer, then a "cable man," and eventually rose to cable foreman.

Carolyn Malkin recalled, "Both my great-grandfather and my grandfather worked for the telephone company from the beginning of telephones, and my grandmother was a long distance telephone operator, and that's how my grandparents met." Bob married Ella

Mae Stull of Canton, N.Y., in the fall of 1904. Carolyn also added an anecdote about one of the highlights of Bob's career: "Grandpa was the American engineer who supervised the laying of the first telephone cable across Sweden, which is how they [Bob and his family] came to live in Sweden for two years. They followed the cable across as it was laid." That project started in September 1920, while Bob worked for International Western Electric Company. They were contracted to run the first cable between Stockholm and Goteborg, some four hundred miles. Bob was the consulting engineer on the project and supervised the laying of the cable.

Bob and Ella had two daughters, Ruth in 1905 and Helen in 1907, and unlike most parents of that era, they challenged their girls to set their sights high.

"Without a doubt," Carolyn stressed, "[Bob's] influence on his children was huge. His emphasis on becoming all one can be, intellectually and physically, made an immense impact on the women in my family's history. In a day when society saw women as caretakers of children, housewives, and caregivers to their husbands, my mother [Ruth] and her sister were encouraged to study hard and go to college.

Left to right: Helen and Ruth Gillespie circa 1916 or 1917.

Mother received her bachelor's degree in geology and her master's degree in micro-paleontology from Cornell University. Aunt Helen got her master's at Columbia in New York City. She was the first woman to receive a license to practice architecture in central New York. She joined Merton Granger's firm in Syracuse as a partner, and the firm's name was changed to Granger & Gillespie."

Bob also made sure he shared his appreciation of the outdoors with his daughters. Family camping trips to some of the places that Bob had explored independently were often the main family vacation of the year.

The well organized campsite of a Gillespie and Dunham family vacation circa 1916 or 1917, at Clear Lake (north of Salmon Lake.) From left to right: Alvine Dunham (Ray's wife,) Helen Gillespie, Ella Mae Gillespie, "Buchaca," Bob Gillespie, Ruth Gillespie and Edwin Rockefeller.

A nice catch of brook trout. Left to right: C. G. Wells, James Gillespie (Bob's father) Clarence Seitz and Bob Gillespie during a 1915 trip to Camp Happy on Salmon Lake.

Bob even convinced his father, the senior "telephone man," to accompany him on some of his adventures. The story that follows is about James Gillespie's first fishing trip to the Adirondacks with his son. Bob writes that his father was past sixty, so the trip would have occurred between 1906 and 1910.

Bob's father, James W. Gillespie.

The Trip to Indian George's

Dad was a man past sixty years old and had not been trout fishing for a very considerable number of years, although in his younger days he did a great deal of fishing and used to talk much about it.

Most of his fishing had been done in the streams of Pennsylvania in the hemlock and pine forests before they had been denuded and the country ruined. I came in on the tail end or the last of the big hemlock woods, and Dad and an old uncle who had been all through the Civil War, and a man by the name of Ambrose Hully, an old forty-niner, had put me through quite a course of sprouts and had initiated me into that Fraternity of Nature in due and ancient form. I was very young at the time, but I have always remained a member in good standing.

After I got out of school, I drifted up into New York State and finally became acquainted with the Adirondacks. As I became better acquainted, I transferred my affections from Pennsylvania to New York and got to love the North Woods so well that my wife came very near applying for a divorce and naming the Adirondacks as correspondent.

I had told Dad all about the wonderful country up there, and of the wonderful hunting and fishing trips, and about the curious things to see and the interesting characters that he ought to meet. He always used to listen and sometimes ask a few questions. On one of his visits to my home, I suggested that he go on one of these trips, but he did not enthuse about it and about all I could get out of him was "Oh, we better wait until next spring."

Finally that winter I got him to consent that on the following Decoration Day[4] he would go with me on a trip to Old Indian George's. Indian George was half Saint Regis Indian and half Mohawk Dutchman. He lived in an old abandoned lumber camp in a little log hut that he had fixed up. It was about three miles back in the woods from the railroad on a very fine trout stream. The country west of his camp was green timber and there were several lakes in which were some very fine trout. I knew George very well and had been to his camp many times. I usually took him some grub and a quart or two of whiskey. He did not like whiskey any better than a hungry cat likes milk and he would do more work for a quart of cheap whiskey than he would for a five dollar bill.

As for his camp, about all I can say is that I might have been in a worse place, but I have never been in a dirtier one. It consisted of one room about 15 ft. one way and not over 25 ft. the other. In the one corner there were two bunks, one above the other. They were made of rough boards. The bedding consisted of a couple of old excelsior mattresses and a mass of quilts and blankets that were all of a dirty brown color and looked as if they had been used in a round

4 Decoration Day was the original name for the national Memorial Day holiday.

Old George Perry better known as Indian George and his camp three miles west of Fulton Chain Station in Herkimer County. Moccasin Foot as he is sometimes called can drink more whiskey than any other man I have ever seen. I have stayed in worse places than his camp but I have never been in a dirtier one.

Bob's picture of George Perry and the caption he typed for it.

house to wipe off locomotive engines. I can best describe the beds by saying that one time one of the boys asked George if there were any bed bugs there and he replied "No sir, not a single one, they are all married with large families." He might have also said that the same applied to wood ticks.

Of course, it was not my intention to take Father to this camp to stay overnight and beyond the fact that I had told him about Indian George, and that he had a camp three miles back in the woods, I had said very little about the camp. I had planned the trip so that Father and I could stay at the little hotel out by the railroad and that we would get George to take us to some of the lakes.

Anyone who has ever had anything to do with the Adirondacks knows that about Decoration Day the black flies are most affectionate, and this particular year was no exception.

We had planned the trip so as to get to the little hotel in the late afternoon and put up there for the night. We had a good supper and turned in early, as we expected to get up about 4:00 a.m. Everything so far had been with us, and I could not see why the trip wouldn't be a great success.

We got up the next morning before daylight and got off to a good start. We had had a good breakfast of bacon, eggs, coffee, bread and butter. The old fellow who ran the hotel said that the flies were pretty bad, and when one of those fellows tells you that you can figure that it is so. I had plenty of dope, but the morning was cool and it was just beginning to get daylight so the flies did not bother us for the first half or three quarters of an hour.

After an hour walk we came to the cabin of Indian George, but he was not there and the place was deserted. It was locked, and apparently George had not been there for several days. We set our packs down and proceeded to set up our rods and get ready to fish. I told Dad he'd better dope up pretty well, for the flies were beginning to get thick. The sun was out in good shape and it was going to be a real warm day, and I just knew that we were going to get a lot of trout out of the little stream that ran by the camp.

We went down to the stream and started in. Dad hooked a couple right away, but the flies were something awful. Dad allowed that in all of the years of his life he had never seen anything like it and he began to make unkind remarks about the Adirondacks and tell me that in Pennsylvania they never had such devilish pests. He even got quite personal in his remarks and said something [to the effect] that I had influenced him against his better judgment, etc. Finally he said that he could not possibly stand it a minute longer and that he was going up in the yard of the camp to build a smudge [fire] as he did not want to die right where he was. I put on an extra dose of the fly dope and fished until I had a few nice ones, then decided that I better go back and see how Dad was making out, for I did not want him to think I had quit him altogether.

As I came in sight of the camp through the trees, I could see that Dad had quite a smudge, and as I came a little nearer I also saw old

Indian George coming down the trail. Back of him was one of the blackest colored fellows that I ever saw, and bringing up the rear was another colored fellow who was sort of a yellow copper color. Dad had just spied them and he had a worried look on his face, but as I came out in the yard of the camp Dad look relieved and remarked "Well lad, there are your friends."

As George and his two companions came into the yard of the camp, I saluted him and introduced him to Dad. He shook hands and said he was awful glad we were there and then he said that he wanted us to meet a couple of his friends that had come to visit him and keep house and do the cooking for a few weeks. He remarked that they were not used to the woods and that they had gotten terribly tanned on the way in.

The black fellow's name was Moore and the yellow fellow was Blair. Blair was from the South and was a cook. Moore was a cook in the dining car service on the New York Central, but had gotten a month off for being drunk, and the two had in some way gotten up in the North Country and fell in with George. They all had plenty of grub and were planning on a good time.

—*Bob Gillespie*

In spite of the plague of black flies that Bob and his father were forced to endure, Bob was successful in acclimating his father to the charms of the region enough to ensure that the trip to Indian George's became just the first of many that James Gillespie made with his son to the Adirondacks.

Chapter 6
The First Gillespie Journal

Two unidentified fishermen try their luck from an "unsinkable" raft.
Bob's caption read: The Titanic on Little Simon.

B OB'S FIRST JOURNAL is actually more of a scrapbook—a hodgepodge of maps, picture-postcards and newspaper clippings, interspersed with snapshots and notes from several years' worth of Adirondack trips. The captions date the images to between 1908 and 1915, but there is no connective narrative. Family vacations and outings with his father and friends make up the bulk of the collection. From their matching caps, one assemblage of young men appears to be from the same baseball team. Trout are ubiquitous, as are pictures of the lakes scattered through the Red Horse Chain. Whether Bob visited all of the lakes is left to guesswork.

One trip has more detail than all the others, an interesting journey that Bob made with Ben Hungerford along the Independence River during the fall of 1912. The following is Bob's description of that trip.

Independence River

October 12–17, 1912

Through six miles of green timber, Independence River looks like this.

Clearwater, or Carter as it is now called, is 58 miles above Utica. 1-½ miles west of the station is Independence Lake, the outlet of which flows into Independence River, which is about 30 miles long and flows into the Black River at Pine Grove about 4-½ miles north of Glenfield on the Black River Railroad. Glenfield is 52 miles northwest of Utica.

The topographic maps for the section between the two maps, a distance of 15 miles is not yet made by the government.

On the morning of October 12, 1912, Ben Hungerford and I left Utica at 9:10 a.m. arriving at Clearwater at 11:30. Walked on in to Independence Lake and had dinner there.

Harry Prochell has a beautiful little camp there. There is about $6,000,000 worth of timber land in this section which is owned by the International Paper Co. A bad thunder storm came up, so we stayed overnight.

At 8:50 a.m. on the 13th we started on down the river, following a trail a little to the south. We lost the trail, so took to the bank of the river.

That afternoon we came to a fine camp on the most beautiful pool I ever saw. We stayed in this camp that night.

Top and center: Independence Lake and Ben Hungerford. Above and left: The big pool on Independence River and the camp near the pool where we stayed.

Below the dam at the foot of the flow grounds.

On the 14th we came on down the river and out of the green timber into a section which had been lumbered. We passed through some very interesting country and saw many deer and lots of partridges. We finally came to a long stillwater and at the foot were the remains of an old dam. This was where the logs had been floated down the river. Near the dam was a little hut in which we stayed that night.

The dam tender's camp. Also used by U.S. surveyors.
We stayed here on the night of October 14, 1912.

I'm getting up the nerve to cross the river on a log. Hungerford makes the crossing.

On the morning of the 15th it was quite cold and [there was] a little snow. We left camp at 11:30 and started on a good trail which crossed the river. We finally left [the] trail and followed the river.

The walking got very rough and we only made a few miles. Crossed to the north side of [the] river and at 4 p.m. pitched the little tent after supper [and] turned in.

On the morning of the 16th everything [was] frozen up. We started at 8:15 and only got a short distance before we ran into a big balsam flats. We had to make a detour and then struck a big stream coming into the main stream. We had to cut down a tree across [the] stream so we could get over. We traveled through some of the roughest country I ever saw.

About 2:30 p.m. we came out of the woods into open country at Huckleberry Lake. Passed through Sperryville at 3:30 and on to Chases Lake at 4 p.m.

Mrs. R. D. Pritchard in front of the inn and post office at Chases Lake.

Stayed that night with an R. D. Pritchard. On the 17th [we] walked on to Glenfield, getting there at 12:30, where we had dinner and took [the] afternoon train, getting to Syracuse that evening.

—*Bob Gillespie*

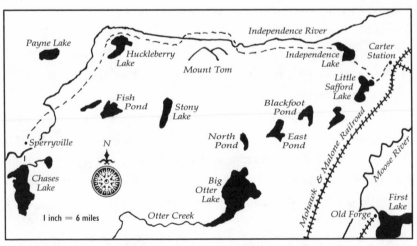

The winding, mostly trailless walk that Bob and Ben made was about 23 miles to Chases Lake with another 10 miles along the road to catch a train outside of Glenfield.

Scenes from Beaver River
& the Lakes Along the
Red Horse Trail

1913–1915

Above: The Hotel Norridgewock (left) is one of the few buildings in sight on arrival at Beaver River Station. Below, left to right standing, are Joe Burk, Ray Dunham, Burt Darrow, Dick Brennan, the Station Agent and Tommy Murtaugh seated in the front.

The wagon road leads away from Beaver River Station, passing the Beaver River Hotel (top) and heads down to the inn at Grassy Point (center.) Bottom: A train pulling into Beaver River Station.

*A boat ride or a
hike to the fire
tower were both
popular activities
at Stillwater and
Beaver River.
Left: Alvine
Dunham stands
at the edge of the
Beaver River Flow
at low water.*

Left: Looking north on Salmon Lake from Wilder's Camp Happy dock.
Middle: The bridge on the way to Trout Pond.
Bottom: Willys Lake.

LITTLE ROCK LAKE

Left to right, top: Fritz Neu, Joe Zahn, Sam Mills & Bob Gillespie. Center: Fritz and Joe at Burt Darrow's camp. Bottom: Clarence and Jess Seitz.

Top: Guides and hunters from the Rap-Shaw Camp on Witchopple Lake return with a bear. Center: The Rap-Shaw camp run by Jimmy Wilder. Right: Jimmy Wilder at an open camp on Big Crooked Lake.

Top: On the porch of Camp Happy, May 16, 1915, (left to right) Dr. Ford Eastman, James Gillespie, C. G. Wells, S. E. Stanton and Jess Seitz. Center: (left) Dr. Ford Eastman and (right) Arthur L. Fox fishing from the Camp Happy dock. Left: Camp Happy.

Top: (left to right) Dr. Ford Eastman, James Gillespie, C. G. Wells, S. E. Stanton & Bob Gillespie. Right: (left to right) F. J. Chesterman, Elmer Wilder and J. R. Lane, June 2, 1913. Below: A quiet moment at Beaver River Station.

Chapter 7
Elmer Wilder

FOR BOB GILLESPIE, Elmer Wilder was not only a fine host as the proprietor of Camp Happy, but also exactly the sort of man that Bob wanted to be around when it came to anything to do with the woods. Elmer was widely known as having acquired the skills necessary to live as he chose—subsistence hunting and fishing, providing guide services and running his little inn. Elmer's self-sufficiency and unassuming manner garnered the respect of "city folk" like Bob that may have bordered on awe.

During the summer months when Bob visited, Elmer often had his family there, his wife Alice (Hubert) and their three daughters, Flora,

Left to right: Grace, Flossie and Flora Wilder.
Previous page: Elmer Wilder during an October 1912 hunt.

Grace and Flossie. They stayed on as long as the weather or the bugs or the guests were hospitable enough for young ladies to be around; otherwise they retreated to a little place in the hamlet of Crystal Dale, about ten miles east of Lowville on the Number Four Road and a little closer to civilization.

Elmer never actually owned the land on which Camp Happy was built, but he was allowed to live there freely as a squatter even after the property changed hands several times. Back then there was an understanding that a man like Elmer was beneficial to the owner simply by acting in his own best interest. While routinely patrolling his hunting and fishing grounds he would also be on the lookout for timber thieves, but his most important job was that of fire spotter, to extinguish or report blazes before they could take off and burn out of control. To the owner of the invaluable virgin timber still standing north of the Beaver River, nothing would be as devastating as a forest fire. A burned acre was worth virtually nothing. For his services (or mere presence on the land) the owner even looked the other way when Elmer added additional guest cottages for his growing clientele.

Over the twenty years starting around 1895, Bob was partly responsible for Elmer's boom in business. Over that time he brought his father, brother, wife, daughters and all his willing friends up to Camp Happy. He brought his father's friends too.

Having enjoyed the hospitality of Elmer and his family so many times, Bob had an idea. He decided to return the favor to Elmer by inviting him and his family to enjoy a few nights in "the big city"—Syracuse! After a pow-wow with his wife and daughters, Elmer agreed, and on February 24, 1915, the family was on their way to the bustling metropolis. Somehow, a writer for the *Post-Standard* Newspaper was tipped off to the scoop, which resulted in three newspaper accounts. The first follows:

Mr. and Mrs. Elmer Wilder and their daughters (left to right) Grace, Flossie and Flora.

Come Out of Adirondacks for First Time in Lives to See the Sights of City

Behold With Astonishment Trolley Cars, Elevators, Theaters and "Skyscrapers."

Mr. and Mrs. Elmer Wilder, born and brought up in the depths of the Adirondacks, have in the last three days been on a pilgrimage which has opened their eyes to a new world. In three days they have seen the accomplishment of a life desire. For the first time they have: Ridden on a street car, seen and ridden on an elevator, watched men at work on a typewriter, been to a moving picture play, seen a theatrical production, watched the process of making a newspaper, inspected a telephone exchange, seen a "skyscraper"—and many other things which had been denied them until this week.

The call of the city to the Wilders—and their three daughters, Flora, Grace and Flossie—came with the advent of city sportsmen several years ago during the camping season along the Beaver River. In winter the Wilders have lived at Crystal Dale, ten miles from Lowville, and in summer they have gone Northward to the river, even further from civilization.

Invited to City.

But during those summers they have made many friends among Syracuse and Utica hunters and campers. And as they are naturally hospitable themselves, their kindness to summer guests brought many invitations to "come to the city and stop with us a while." The idea grew, until after a year of planning, Mr. and Mrs. Wilder decided to accept an invitation from Robert M. Gillespie of the New York Telephone Company to visit Syracuse. As a result, one of the biggest adventures in the lives of Mr. and Mrs. Wilder—and certainly the biggest adventure in the lives of the little Wilders—began Monday, when they came southward from Lowville, and saw a modern city for the first time. Little time was spent in Utica. The main object of the trip was to see the sights of Syracuse under the direction of Mr. and Mrs. Gillespie.

Everything "Fine!"

Laconic, modest and accepting the new wonders of the world with the nonchalance of a man city bred, Mr. Wilder has but one word for everything—"fine!"

The little Wilders have been just as shyly interested in the street cars, the electric lights, the paved streets and the roar of traffic.

Nothing palls on them, because before one miracle is over another begins. But there have been some tired little Wilders at nightfall.

"There is so MUCH of everything, and we have SEEN so much that we can't tell what we like best," they said yesterday. "But it will be pretty nice to get back home away from the noise." "Which do you like better, Utica or Syracuse?" Mr. Wilder was asked. "Syracuse," he said. "There's more of it." Which, perhaps, struck the keynote of the entire party.

Treat for Mrs. Wilder.

Yesterday Mr. Wilder was taken to the Franklin Automobile Works, while his wife, in a personally directed tour by Mrs. Gillespie, made the rounds of those institutions dearest to woman's heart— the department stores. The moving stairway in one shop attracted much attention. "It's much nicer than an elevator," said Mrs. Wilder, "because it doesn't go so fast and doesn't give you that queer feeling." The moving picture shows were one of the first goals of the travelers. The darkness at first overawed the little Wilders, and even had its effect upon their father, who jokingly hesitated about "going into a cavern." Late in the afternoon Mr. and Mrs. Wilder were taken through the Post-Standard Building, and the operation of publishing a newspaper from reporter's "copy" to the mailing room was explained to them. "I never knew there was so much work to getting out a newspaper before," said Mr. Wilder as he left the building.

Go to Shows.

Beaver River hours differ from those in Syracuse. Neither Mr. nor Mrs. Wilder was allowed to go to bed early last night. In the first place, Mr. Wilder's friends were determined that he should see a burlesque show before he went back home. Mrs. Wilder's friends were equally determined that she should see a vaudeville performance.

Accordingly, the couple were separated for a few hours, and while Mr. Wilder was sitting in K-1 at the Bastable, Mrs. Wilder

The Erie Canal at Salina Street in downtown Syracuse, N.Y.,
when Erie Boulvard was still the Erie Canal. Circa 1904.

was enjoying the bill at the Temple Theater. And it was all enjoyable, because it was "lights and music, and gayety, and noise," the stuff big cities are made of.

Today there will be more shopping expeditions, and more sight-seeing. For one thing, the family is going to the top of the highest building in Syracuse, and from there get a panoramic picture of the city in its entirety. Then there will be movies, and more street car rides, and more trips in automobiles.

Return Home Tomorrow.

The expedition comes to an end tomorrow, for on that day the Wilders leave for home—home in the Adirondacks, which is so much better, in the end, because it IS home, and because it is away from the hurry and noise, and trouble, and dirt. In fact, Mr. Wilder remarked in a whisper last night that he knows now why city men like to get up in the hills and woods once in a while—something he never understood before.

The next day's story began,

Adirondack Guide is Lost Where Trees Have No Moss

Elmer Wilder Cannot Tell Directions in Streets of Syracuse—Tiring of Noise and Bustle, He Longs for the Quiet of the Big Woods.

"There is one thing about the city that bothers me quite a lot," said Elmer Wilder, the Adirondack guide, last night. This is the longest speech Mr. Wilder has made since he came to Syracuse Tuesday to see a city for the first time in his life.

The thing that bothers him is that he has completely lost his sense of direction. In the woods Mr. Wilder can instinctively go north or south through trackless forests, over hills and across streams without losing his way. He knows instinctively where to go, how to go and when to go. But in the city he confesses himself as hopelessly lost as a city man would be in the heart of the mountains.

Not that he can't explain it easily. This is his explanation: "The trees in the city here haven't got any moss on 'em, and you can't tell which is north and which is south!'"

Leave for Home Today.

Mr. and Mrs. Wilder, with their three children, leave at noon today for Crystal Dale after four days' adventure. They are thoroughly tired out, and for the last twenty-four hours Mr. Wilder has had a sort of hunger in himself for the woods. He wants to get away from the noise.

Yesterday was a busy day for the sight-seers. Friends of Mr. Wilder, men who have been guided by him year after year in the North Country, called on R. M. Gillespie, who has been entertaining Mr. Wilder this week, to invite the guide to different points of interest in the city.

E. L. French of the Crucible Steel Company was one of the first to call upon him after finding that he was in the city. As a result, Mr. Wilder spent an enjoyable morning inspecting the steel plant.

The next ones to offer their services as "guides," were Charles L. Stone and Douglas E. Petit of the Onondaga County Savings Bank. Mr. Wilder was taken through the bank, and was highly impressed by the sight of $35,000 in real cash. He stopped to figure how long it would take him to earn that amount, and "allowed he'd have to pack every day for thirty years at $3 a day to earn that much."

The third article headlined "Return to the Woods" reported, "Mr. Wilder, under the influence of the last four days spent in factories, shops, big buildings and street cars, became slightly more talkative than usual as he was preparing to leave.

"There's two things that I might say about the city," he said. "In the first place, while it's all right for some people to live here, I don't see how they can stand the noise.

"The second thing is that I don't see what use people have for street cars. The walking is good, and you have nice sidewalks. So what's the use of riding?

"We never were treated so fine in our lives, and we've got something to remember forever. We've seen more than we ever expected to see, and I guess we didn't see everything here at that. But just the same, we all feel just a little tired out, and we'll be glad to get back home again."

Their return to the Adirondacks might have seemed like a drift backward in time, the din and lights of the city slowly dimming behind them as the numbers of people and dwellings shrank. The snow got deeper. Nature got closer. The sounds of woodpeckers hammering and the silence of the night welcomed them back home. The city did not have the draw they favored.

Chapter 8

The Dunham Boys

R AY DUNHAM FIRST APPEARS in Bob's journals in March of 1914, wearing snowshoes and carrying a long pole, apparently to help survive a potential fall through the thinning ice of March. Once he appears, Ray is a steadfast fixture throughout the rest of the journals, a good-humored friend to Bob and a reliable woodsman.

Ray's full name was Raymond Franklin Dunham and he was born on September 26, 1884. His younger brother Harvey Leslie was born on October 6, 1887. The Dunham boys were the sons of Franklin and Flora M. Jones Dunham of Sauquoit, N.Y. Harvey wasn't around in Bob's first journal, but after their meeting on Salmon Lake, Bob and Harvey's friendship took off.[5]

[5] That meeting is described in Harvey's poem on page 4 of this book.

Ray and Harvey were 16 and 13 years old respectively when the first record of their travels to the Adirondacks made the local newspaper. An announcement appeared in the *Utica Sunday Journal* in July, 1901, that read, "Rev. A. L. Byron-Curtiss of Rome, Rev. A. E. Dunham of Camden and [his nephews] Masters Raymond and Harvey Dunham,

Harvey Dunham with the long pole he used to propel an old dugout canoe while his brother Ray (left page) used his pole as a precautionary device, to lay across the ice if it gave way under him.

are occupying the former's camp, known heretofore as the Bennett Camp at North Lake. Mr. Byron-Curtiss, having purchased his camp, is making notable improvements, among them being the addition of a kitchen and dining room on the rear, and a porch on the lake side. He has renamed the renovated cottage Nat Foster Lodge."

It was common for notices of local goings-on to make the broadsheet back then, especially if the participants had attained some local celebrity. Both ministers had served as rectors of Christ Church in Forestport and the Rev. A. L. Byron-Curtiss was the author of the popular book *The Life and Adventures of Nat Foster, Trapper and Hunter of the Adirondacks,* released in 1897. The book, with its hair-raising stories of Continental Army battles and close calls with panthers, wolves and

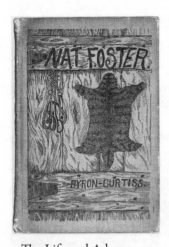

The Life and Adventures of Nat Foster, Trapper and Hunter of the Adirondacks, *by A. L. Byron-Curtiss, published in 1897.*

Indians provided plenty of tall tales for the folklorist-preacher to tell around a roaring campfire. And those stories may have left a particular impression on young Harvey Dunham. Fifty years later Harvey would publish his own book of Adirondack folklore, the classic *Adirondack French Louie: Early Life in the North Woods*, and it's quite possible that Harvey first heard about the hermit-lumberjack he would later immortalize around the campfire at Nat Foster Lodge.

Rev. Byron-Curtiss made sure to include a note about the Dunhams' visit to North Lake in his Nat Foster Lodge log book:

July 10, 1901: Rev. Andrew E. Dunham of Camden, N.Y. and Byron-Curtiss of Rome and Masters Raymond and Harvey Dunham, nephews of Rev. Dunham, arrived and opened camp at 11:30 a.m. having started from Forestport by special rig. They were much delayed at the Mohawk and Malone Railroad Station in getting provisions out of the freight house. Water in lake very high. Weather pleasant.

Did Harvey first learn about French Louie from Byron-Curtiss? We may never know, but it's hard to imagine that the woods-loving minister didn't spark Harvey's curiosity. Many of the larger-than-life characters that Byron-Curtiss knew and wrote about eventually made it to the pages of Harvey's book half a century later.

Throughout the next fifty years Ray and Harvey remained friends with Rev. Byron-Curtiss. They visited each others' camps, relished fresh trout dinners, downed bottles of "liquid bait" and emptied pouches of tobacco as they enjoyed the age-old ritual of story-telling. And Rev. Byron-Curtiss had some good ones!

"There was one particular backwoods hamlet," he began, "where a majority of the woodsmen were bald. A dynamic hair tonic peddler from Utica resolved to profit from this sad situation, so he mixed up a batch of his most powerful potion, packed it in boxes and started on his wagon trip north. On his way the weather

The Reverend A. L. Byron-Curtiss and Nat Foster Lodge.

turned awful and soon one of those terrible Adirondack thunderboomers was upon him. While on the bridge over Black River the salesman's steed spooked at a close-by thunder-clap and immediately broke into a dash. With a jerk on the reins and a yell, the salesman tried to slow the terrified horse, but it was too late. The animal slipped on the wet planks and the wagon slid sideways, hitting the rail, and the tonic flew out of the wagon box. The jars smashed with a clatter and the potent liquid cascaded into the river.

"I don't recall exactly how long after the accident it happened, but I do know that the fishermen there developed a novel technique. Forestporters would stake out their favorite spot carrying a miniature red and white striped pole, barber shears, and razor. They would place the barber pole in the shallows and cry out: 'Get your free hair cut and trim here!' The trout, whose hair had grown too long beat a path right out of the water and were picked up by the inventive anglers. It wasn't until the flood of April 1869, when the dam at North Lake gave out, that the waters muddied, making it impossible for the fish to see the barber poles, and the practice died out."

Camp life meant good times. That much we know.

Chapter 9
Camp Happy No More

Elmer Wilder's Camp Happy on Salmon Lake.

URING THE SECOND WEEK OF MAY 1915, Bob Gillespie returned to Camp Happy with his father and some friends. Little did they know the trip would be their last opportunity to enjoy the comforts that the camp and its proprietor had provided them for years.

As a harbinger of what was to come, this article ran in the *Journal and Republican*, Lowville, N.Y., on November 18, 1915:

Must Skidoo.

All Persons Who Occupy State Land in the Adirondacks and Elsewhere to be Forced Off.

Albany, Nov. 17—All persons occupying State land must show cause why they should not be ousted and all permanent structures on State property must be removed is the sweeping order issued by

Conservation Commissioner George D. Pratt. Formal notice of the commissioner's intention to enforce the law is being served as fast as possible upon 700 alleged trespassers, and his legal adviser, Marshall McLean, is preparing the necessary papers to enforce the sweeping order. Notable legal battles are expected, as this order will affect many wealthy campers who for years enjoyed choice portions of the people's domain. Among those affected are Colonel Mann, editor of Town Topics, who has long had a magnificent residence on an island in Lake George; State Historian Golden, who has a camp on an island in the narrows of that lake, and the estate of Edward Ellis, who built a handsome cabin on Uncas Island in the lake some years ago.

In the Adirondacks there are very many valuable camps, especially in the vicinity of Raquette and Saranac Lakes, which are included in the alleged occupancy of State land.

An effort to provide for the leasing of these camp sites failed in the constitutional convention after a vigorous fight and Commissioner Pratt says he intends to enforce the law as he finds it without fear or favor.

More than twenty years had passed since "forever wild" had been added to the state Constitution, a period of time New York spent in legal and political turmoil over the enforcement of the amendment. In 1915, however, newly elected Governor Charles Whitman proposed changes to the Conservation Law that included the appointment of a single executive to lead it. When the changes were approved, Gov. Whitman tapped George D. Pratt for the job. He was a wealthy idealist with executive experience and there may have been no better person suited to undertake the unseemly acts of eviction and destruction called for by the amendment's definition. Commissioner Pratt was unable to be influenced by money or politics and as the former president of the Camp Fire Club of America he brought a conservationist's enthusiasm for what had been considered distasteful in the eyes of many. He managed the "squatter problem" with tact and judiciousness, settling over seven hundred of nearly a thousand cases. By mid-1916, mansions and hovels, log cottages and cathedrals of Adirondack architecture were all scheduled for the torch, Elmer Wilder's camp and cottages included.

In the years since the state acquired Camp Happy and the 75,377 acres surrounding it to settle their lawsuit with Dr. Webb, they had tolerated Elmer's presence, but no longer. An article in the March 15, 1916, *Lowville Journal and Republican* contained the final warning the Wilders and other squatters, rich and poor, would receive in the mail.

Last Call to Vacate.

Final and Drastic Action to be Taken Against 255 Occupants of State Land.

Albany, March 15—Last call to vacate State land, before final and drastic action is taken by the Conservation Commission, is contained in a letter just mailed by Conservation Commissioner George D. Pratt to 255 occupants of State land who have thus far failed to respond to his endeavors to secure an amicable adjustment of the squatter situation. Out of 790 cases on record the first of last November, according to a statement by the commission, these are the only ones in which no progress has yet been made. In the last four months 265 cases have been "completely closed," says the statement. Fifty-nine occupants have signed stipulations agreeing to move within a reasonable time. Forty-two owners of tent platforms have promised to take out permits under regulations prescribed by the Commission and to donate "their platforms" to the State. Sixty-five other cases are in correspondence, while 104 occupants stand pat in a determination to fight through the courts.

"If you have any statements to make the Commission will accept a reply within ten days." says Commissioner Pratt to the 255 who have failed to reply. "There is no question" he continues, "about the full enforcement of this policy. The absolute conditions are that all unlawful occupancy of State lands shall cease at the earliest practicable date, that no favoritism will be shown, and that all parties will be treated in a similar manner."

"The situation," says the Commissioner, "is simply that the Constitution provides that lands belonging to the State within the Adirondack and Catskill Parks shall be forever kept as wild forest lands, and shall not be leased, sold or exchanged, or taken by any person or corporation. This provision, as construed by several Attorney-Generals, prohibits anything except the temporary use of these State lands. . . .

"The Department desires first of all the co-operation of all concerned," continues Commissioner Pratt. "I regret very much that this situation should exist or that any person should suffer any hardship. But, on the other hand, I intend honestly to live up to my oath of office and uphold and enforce the laws and constitution of the State, and am therefore compelled to act as outlined in this letter. I desire to be as fair with occupants as possible and where it is deemed to be to the public interest, and under the advice of the Attorney-General, the Commission is willing to consider offers from occupants for the removal of their buildings from State lands, provided they vacate promptly. Otherwise the Commission has authority to remove buildings from State land, or to destroy them if necessary."

In October 1916, the wait was over. Lowville's *Journal and Republican* reported that "Elmer Wilder spent a few days last week at Stillwater, returning Saturday with some of his camp furniture from Salmon Lake. Mr. Wilder removed the equipage from the camp he had occupied summers for the past twenty years at Stillwater before the State officials burned the camps in that section." Camp Happy was no more.

Chapter 10
Marriage, Heartbreak, and War

To COMPLETELY TELL THE STORY of our fledgling woodsman and future author Harvey Dunham, we need to step back in time briefly to a tragic period in his life, shortly after he was married. These events occurred before Harvey befriended Bob Gillespie, but they are part of his biography and ought to be shared.

In August of 1912, twenty-four-year-old Harvey Dunham was wed to Bessie Throop of Sauquoit, N.Y. Bessie was a kind woman from a fine family. About a year after the nuptials the couple announced that they were expecting their first child. On May 23, 1914, Bessie bore a healthy daughter, Jean Margaret, but became ill from complications from the delivery. Bessie never recovered. On June 12 she died at home. For Harvey, one love was brought into his life as another one slipped away. This *Waterville Times* article captured a sense of the tragedy experienced by the entire community:

> The sad news of the death of Bessie May Throop, wife of Harvey L. Dunham, which occurred at her home in Albany, Friday, June 12, came as a thunderbolt from a clear sky to her large circle of friends. Mrs. Dunham was born in this village 24 years ago, the daughter of Medville J. and Nettie Throop. She was married in 1912 to Harvey Dunham. She was educated in the schools here and was a member of the M. E. Church and always took an active part in the Sunday school and Epworth league. She was also for sometime organist of the church. She was a young woman of a beautiful character, kind disposition and one who retained as long as she lived the many friends she made who are deeply grieved and will mourn her. Besides her husband, Mrs. Dunham is survived by an infant daughter, Jean Margaret, her father, M. J. Throop of this place, and one brother, Raymond, of Newark, NJ.

August 7, 1912 the M. E. Church was filled with friends who witnessed the marriage of the happy young couple who were starting their new life together, which was brought to a close so soon, and caused the same church again on Monday to be filled with mournful friends.

Harvey must have realized that he was in no shape to care for his infant daughter alone. With the counsel of his parents and his younger sister Florence, he decided that they were better suited to the responsibilities of raising Jean, whom they accepted into their loving care.

With those difficult arrangements made, Harvey joined the Merchant Marines, for war had broken out in Europe. Talk was flying that the U.S. would be drawn in; joining the Merchant Marines may have been preferable to being drafted as an infantryman.

While these are the facts of Harvey's young adulthood, it's impossible to know his thoughts and feelings as he adjusted to the loss of his wife. For Seaman Dunham, ocean swells and the threat of enemy ships were probably welcome distractions from a simple life that had turned suddenly dark.

Harvey remained in service through the duration of World War I and received a furlough shortly after hostilities ceased. On Christmas Day 1918, Harvey returned to stand with his brother Ray at his wedding to Alvine Hempel of Cranford, N.J.

By the following summer, Harve (as he then liked to be known) had been honorably discharged from the Merchant Marines. He was preparing to head back to the woods again. Ray, Bob Gillespie and Jessie Seitz were planning a trip in August. The plan was to rendezvous at Beaver River Station by train with all their gear. From there, their destination would be Salmon Lake, to see what was left of their old haunt, Camp Happy. Their next two weeks of camping and exploring were recorded in Bob's Second Journal.

Chapter 11
The Red Horse Chain

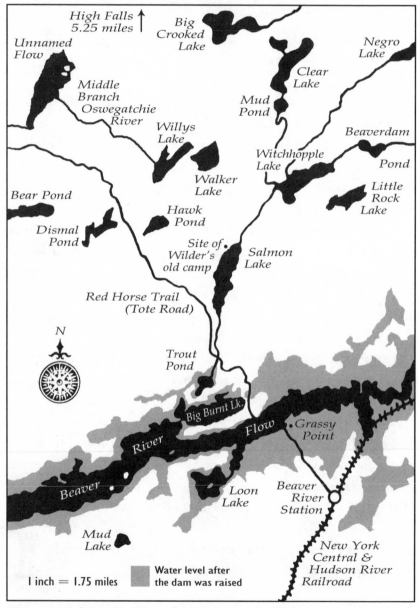

The caption below Bob's map read: "The new flow line after the pirates got through with the work of destruction," referring to the rise in the level of the Beaver River.

The Second Trip Journal of Bob Gillespie
with Harve Dunham, Ray Dunham and Jess Seitz
August 16, 1919–August 31, 1919

Saturday, August 16, 1919

Ray Dunham, Jess Seitz and Bob Gillespie started from Syracuse at 3 p.m. on New York Central Local—(no first-class train would carry them)—arrived in Utica at 5 p.m. Harve Dunham left Albany at 12:55; arrived in Utica at 3:20. The whole bunch met in front of Bell Telephone Office at 11:15 p.m. Got the tent and some other traps out of the office and took them down to the New York Central Station at 12 midnight.

Sunday, August 17th

After a little lunch and witnessing a near scrap between a Canadian and a Jew, took the bunch of duffel and got on the 2:15 a.m. train at 2:10. Train finally pulled out at 2:40. Arrived at Fulton Chain at 4:45, when we run into a rain storm. Harve butted into a bunch of girls and bummed a handout from one named Dot Knapp. They were going to 7th Lake and got off at Carter. Finally arrived at Beaver River at just daylight and at 5:30. It was a dark morning, but it had not rained there at all.

The four of us explored about and inspected the whole place until 6:30, when Pop Bullock opened up his hotel, including the Post Office. We ordered breakfast for four, which was prepared by Deliah, and was ready a little after 7 o'clock. We also dug up Lu Beach, who runs the wagon to the river at 9 o'clock. We found the canoe at the river. Also, we met Burt Darrow there who was on his way to Burnt Lake with a party.

"Pop" Bullock and Deliah at the inn.

Grassy Point—Start of the trip, Aug. 17 1919.

Ray put Harve and Bob across the river with the two heavy packs and they started over the tote road, getting to Salmon Lake at 11:25 a.m. The lake through the trees sure looked good.

Salmon Lake as it appeared through the trees. Oh Boy!

Ray and Jess took canoe and the duffel and went down river via Big Burnt to the landing for Trout Pond. The river was very low and they had to unload and carry over the muck into Big Burnt, getting to the landing at 1 p.m. In the meantime, Harve and Bob came back to Trout

The camp through the trees.

Pond and over to Big Burnt, getting there just ahead of Ray and Jess. The bunch toted the stuff to Trout, across Trout, and at 4:15 p.m. had the canoe and all but two of the big boxes up to Salmon. Harve and Jess went on up Salmon to establish the camp, and Ray and Bob went back to Trout Pond for the last two loads.

Before going to Trout Pond, they sneaked a rod, line and six worms. When they arrived at Trout Pond, they shoved the little boat out and tried fishing. The day had been cloudy with just a little shower or two, and also a little wind—just ideal for trout. The result was 12 fine trout in 30 minutes; the largest 12" long. This was on six worms. Then the two toted the last of the duffel up to Salmon and took the canoe on up the lake to camp, where Harve and Jess had set up the tent, made some beds of spruce, and got everything in ship-shape. Then there was some big eats and the bunch turned in at 10 p.m. all in.

                            "B" [Bob]

Monday August 18th

Rained most of the night—at least it was agreed that it did—but no one stayed awake to see. It was raining at 8 a.m. when we turned out, but let up very soon and we had a fine breakfast of trout, bacon, coffee, bread and jelly. It was then agreed that Harve and Jess should go to Trout Pond and Ray and Bob should fix up the camp and put things in the best possible shape.

After Harve and Jess got down the lake, Ray and Bob washed up the dishes, cut a little wood and then took an old boat, as Harve and Jess had the canoe, and first went to the old Smith camp. There they found a couple of old saw-horses and a piece or two of stove pipe. Then they went to the old Townsend Camp and found all kinds of valuables, including a perfectly good table, a two-hole box stove, a pail, tea pot, a big board, two pieces of flat iron, stove pipe, a National Biscuit can, which makes a dandy oven, and a lot of little odd things that we could use in camp. The two went over to the old Cobb Camp and found two old homemade tables that Elmer had formerly had, a nice big pan, a bottle of kerosene, a coffee pot, a crosscut saw, a big piece of old canvas, a box of spuds, some onions, and a few boards. Then they loaded the stuff in the boat and went over to the Townsend Camp and picked up that outfit and came across the lake to camp. The boat was pretty low in the water and great care had to be used in getting the old boat safe to the landing, but it was finally accomplished without mishap.

Then the table was set up, four poles cut and a canopy made and the old canvas used to cover it. The stove was set up and a real camp made.

There was a little shower or two that bothered some, but Ray and Bob figured it would help Jess and Harve out in the fishing.

About 4 p.m. Jess and Harve showed up and sure were surprised at all the stuff in camp and the arrangement of same. They opened up their fish basket and had a few nice trout. They also brought back some boxes which were nailed to trees for cupboards. They also brought back one box which Ray and Bob did not notice at first, but finally when the last of the things were being picked up, Bob started to pick up the odd box and had the surprise of his life. It seems that Harve and Jess had phenomenal luck in Trout Pond and had put the biggest fish in the box with leaves, and a few small ones in the basket. Bob yelled to Ray to look in the box. When the fish were

Putting the finishing touches on the camp—Ray always was a good fellow around camp.

Left to right: Harve, Bob and Ray.
Harve tells all about the 14½" trout. Bob and Ray don't believe a word of it.
Right: One hour's catch by Harve and Jess. Largest 1½ pounds.

taken out there were twenty four of them and they weighed seven pounds. The longest was fourteen and a half inches long.

It was sure some fine catch of trout. Harve and Jess said they caught them in a little more than an hour, but Ray and Bob would not believe it.

Anyway, it was a fine mess of fish and then the bunch started in to prepare supper.

After some awful big eats, the gang turned in at 10 p.m.

It had been a dark cloudy day and quite a little rain mixed in, but the tent was tight and a big fire in front of it made things very comfortable. Then too, with luck coming our way and lots of fish ahead, it was only a few minutes before the gang was dead to the world.

"B" [Bob]

Tuesday, August 19th

Talk about going light—nothing doing. We filled one end of the coach with our duffel of which 9/10 at least was grub; we worked all day Sunday getting it into camp and now by gosh we're getting away with it in great style, and now, while Ray gets the big fire started and Bob sings a song about a gentleman named McGraw, John McGraw, who did not care at all, and Jess gets oatmeal ready for the morning, I'll try to tell what happened yesterday.

We got up in the morning with Bob standing over us with a fiery cross yelling bloody murder. That was about 7:30. To tell what we had for breakfast would take too long. We washed the breakfast dishes and then Bob and Ray took the canoe and went to Trout Pond. Of course they had to go to Trout Pond and fish in the same hole where Jess and Harve made their famous catch. That sure was some—well, Bob wrote all about that, but that's right, they caught them in a little over an hour, and—Oh, My God!

They, Bob and Ray, went to Trout Pond and Jess and Harve with camera, gun and fish rods followed the telephone line to the inlet. The gun was for red squirrels, not venison, but it's a darn lucky thing for two ducks that they saw or heard that .22 in time to make their getaway.

At the inlet, Jess pulls out a seven-inch trout and Harve goes back in the woods with the .22 and misses a couple of squirrels. He says they were way the H— and gone up in the top of a big pine tree—Maybe they were, who knows?

Then, Jess comes to the landing with his little troutlet and Harve meets him there squirrel-less, and together they raised a sunken boat and paddled back to camp. The boat they believed was one of Elmer's—Elmer Wilder—everybody knows Elmer. They were back to camp about fifteen minutes when a hard thunderstorm came up. One flash made the telephone wire, which went only a few inches over the tent, snap like a machine gun. The rain came down in torrents. The dead limbs began to fall as the wind increased. Looking out from the tent, they could just make out the lower end of the lake. Smoke was

Harve looking for squirrels.

coming up from a camp on Mrs. Cobb's site, and they figured that Ray and Bob were there, later to find out that they were on the trail and under the canoe during the storm. Soon after the storm, Harve and Jess began the preparation of supper and endeavored to make it one which would appeal to a couple of water-soaked fisherman. About six o'clock they came in, Ray and Bob, and they did eat that supper as though they wished for nothing more. They had eleven trout—most of them very nice ones. They caught them in the lower end of the lake and in Trout Pond, and one big one, so Bob says, they chased up and down the outlet—Bob with a big stick and Ray with a net—up and down the stream and over the rocks and they got him cornered in a dry place in the stream where they captured him. Another one Ray hooked while fishing in the lake near Mrs. Cobb's, but did not land him. The hook, no doubt, pierced the poor trout's brain and, according to Ray, there was a great splashing on the port or starboard side of the canoe, whatever it is, and they saw a big trout making great circles on the surface of the water. Ray sat in the bow with the net and Bob took the paddle and took after him. Back and forth across the lake they went at full speed, following the fancy curves of the loco trout. Bob didn't say anything about the canoe taking the swells made by the trout, but that's because he didn't think of it. Anyway, so they say, and one vouches for the other, after a strenuous chase they managed to net the speeding hydroplane of a loco trout. After that, they were all in, and went directly back to camp to tell about it.

Around the campfire that evening, Jess told us how the salt got in the ocean and there were other stories told too—but—well, the stars came out and we all agreed the rainy season was over. Then, with a big fire throwing plenty of heat into the camp, we turned in and the man who got to sleep first didn't have to lie awake and listen to the other three snoring which—Oh, My God! It's awful.

"H" [Harve]

Wednesday, August 20th

Did not open bright and fair, but kept up the good record and opened up dark and lowery, same as all the days so far. However, beyond a few spatters in the early forenoon, no rain materialized, and ourselves and camp gave up a certain amount of unwelcome moisture—not all by a lot, but enough to make things more comfortable. After breakfast, at the ladylike hour of 8:30 with trout for the centerpiece, as usual, Harvey and Jess set out in the canoe down the lake with Trout Pond for an objective, probably with the idea of duplicating their catch of Monday, but how their average suffered you will find out later. Bob and Ray, having cleaned up the necessary camp chores, took the boat belonging to the Witchhopple gang, which we had borrowed, and set out up the inlet taking the rods and the .22 to be primed for any and all occasions. On the way up Bob, with the fry pan in mind, cut short the existence of a few frogs, blowing them some twelve or fifteen feet in the air with a shot judiciously placed under their yellow bellies, and also annexed a trout from beside the big rock.

Leaving the boat at the landing, they went along up the stream, fishing a bit here and there and gathering in about half a dozen more for the larder. Then, inasmuch as frogs legs are a pleasant variation from a steady trout diet, they decided to hit for Little Rock Pond, but the trail, evidently not used for some years, soon petered out to less than the proverbial squirrel track, and they plowed along in sort of hit or miss fashion for some fifteen or twenty minutes, finally striking the lake at the upper end which was exactly as they "orter."

Harve on the way to Trout Pond.

To their surprise and disgust as well, they found that beaver had built a dam at the outlet and raised the water level some two or three feet, making a rotten shoreline where once there had been a good one. The beaver house was nearby and was a large one of its kind, standing some eight or ten feet above the level of the water. From its top, Bob caught a sunfish (K.C.), meanwhile speculating upon the probable effect of a few sticks of dynamite placed upon Mr. Beaver's roof and properly urged to action. After disposing of lunch, they said farewell to Little Rock, shedding no tears over Ray's statement that he didn't give a D-m- if he never saw the cussed place again.

On the way back to the landing, a hardly-to-be-suspected spring hole gave up an even half dozen beauties, each about eight inches long. At the landing they bailed out an old scow once belonging to Elmer Wilder, and with a piece of board for a paddle and a can to keep the lake in its place, finally made camp, where they found Jess and Harve awaiting them with supper started, and four trout as the fruit of their Trout Pond fishing expedition; also some darn story about not being able to get the boat on the pond because some man already had it— some fish.

Well, a bang-up good supper made everyone feel right, and a full gut and a big fire sent everybody to the balsam feeling fine.

(Written on a broken box, sitting on a broken chair to the tune of rain drops on a tight roof and the rumble of distant thunder.)

"R" [Ray]

Ray writing the "log."

Thursday, August 21st

While Harvey and Bob are getting breakfast and Ray making up lunches, I'll try and write what transpired yesterday. On the morning of the above date, everybody dressed lightly, and armed with fishing rods and one of Ray's famous lunches, the old trail for Willys Lake was hit via Beaver Meadow and Hawk Pond.

Left to right: Bob, Jess, Ray.
Resting in the tall timber between Salmon Lake and Hawk Pond.

Found the trails fairly good between Elmer's old campsite and Hawk Pond, but from there to Willys Lake it was not good, and a sharp lookout was necessary to keep headed in the right direction. The trip was planned on Wednesday evening, and Ray had the bunch enthused telling about great fishing in Willys Lake. We found, or rather Bob did, a boat in good condition and we all piled into it—everybody having tackle, all set for the grand and glorious feeling that comes to the trout fisherman when the speckled beauty grabs the fly on the first cast. Sorry to relate, nothing like this happened, and Willys Lake was fished in every conceivable manner, but no fish.

Bob and Harvey went down the outlet, but no fish. While they were away, Ray and Jesse had a look at Walker.

A few clouds appeared in the sky and Bob predicted rain, but the rest of the bunch didn't pay much attention to his remarks. They, however, came true—Ray and Jesse were the victims to get soaked. Now, rain doesn't mean very much, but when the only bed you have is hanging on some poles, it is a serious matter to a lot of tired fisherman. Oh, yes, I forgot—on the way over to Willys, Harvey made a remarkable shot. He almost killed a duck. I'm afraid had we to depend on the rifle, we would all go hungry, but this is a fishing trip and a good one. Every day some trout were caught, and this day is no exception as you will presently see.

The return was rather warm walking, but camp loomed in sight at 6:30 and Bob suggested he and Harvey get supper while Ray and Jesse try a favorite spot on Salmon Lake near Cobbs' campsite. Of course, Ray and Jesse were willing, and in spite of wind, rain and a soaking, Ray landed two dandy trout while Jesse was very much put out by a great big bullhead swallowing his bait. The two fishermen returned at seven, and after one of those good meals that Harvey can get up, the bunch turned in, all agreeing that after all, Good Old Salmon Lake is the best of all.

"J" [Jess]

Turning in at 10 P.M. Aug 21st

Friday, August 22nd

Very beautiful day; fog on the lake in early morning, but the sun soon dried it off.

Harve decided to stay in camp, and Ray, Jess and Bob started out for Summit Pond. They could not induce Harve to go, and after accusing him of having a date with "Dot" or some other dame, they left camp in the canoe and paddled up the inlet. They shot a few frogs, caught a few trout and picked some flowers.

When they got to Witchhopple Lake, they found the lake at least three feet higher than normal. Investigation showed that the d--- beaver had built three dams across the outlet and raised old Ned generally. They went up on the trail to Mud Pond and when they got there they found Professor Hartnett and another fellow there with a number of illegal trout which they were preparing to broil. The "other fellow" was making an awful mess of trying to start a fire. Bob had the little axe along so he handed it to the fellow, and with Ray's assistance a fire was started. The three started on and took the boat to Clear Lake and went over to the north side of the lake and there ate lunch. Then they went to the summit and all around the pond looking for frogs, but someone had beat them to it and they got but four. Jess spied a big one up in the woods and, as he said, "feeding up land." Bob came up with the gun and promptly missed a point blank shot. Then the three climbed the crag from above Clear Lake, and from this point for miles and miles is one unbroken virgin forest. It was then and there agreed that the person or persons who desecrated it should be sent to Hell for eternity. Then they came back across Clear to Mud, where the professor and his partner were still fishing the spring hole. They took counsel and decided to take a due east course from Mud Pond and hit the outlet of Negro Lake on Webb's. This they did, it taking just thirty-five minutes to hit the stream. The going was a little rough in spots as there were many rocks. Jess banged his knee, but a little Christian Science on the part of Ray and Bob, and mighty little sympathy thrown in, enabled him to go to it in a minute or two. They

Jess getting a few from a "spring hole."

fished down Negro Lake outlet, picking up a few trout, and finally hit the canoe at the landing at 6:10. They got to camp at 6:30, where they found Harve had prepared all kinds of eats and oh, boy!—how they did lay to it. They found no signs of any visitors having been in camp, and Harve did not volunteer any information, so the dishes were washed, camp cleaned up, a little more wood cut and the bunch turned in at 10:15 under a clear sky filled with stars.

"B" [Bob]

Saturday August 23rd

The mists lay heavy on the lake, the opposite shore being at times completely hidden from view. The coals of last night's big friendship fire still smoldered in the fireplace, but a few kindlings soon brought them to life, and the welcome crackle of the morning fire aroused the later risers and brought them out from under the snug warm blankets—a little drowsy at first, but after a wash in the lake as exhilarated as ever.

While breakfast was in the making, Old Sol appeared over the little mountain across the lake, and the scurrying mists retreated before a gentle southwest breeze. It was the dawn of another day of days. Before breakfast was all cleared away, the itinerary for the day was complete, in that sometime during the day someone or all of us would go to the station for bread and mail.

After several days of roaming about the country exploring new lakes and wetting lines in new streams, it is very enjoyable to just fuss about camp, straightening things up in general and replenishing the ever-vanishing woodpile. Here's where the crosscut saw came in, but as one handle was very loose and a homemade affair at that, Bob decided to put a new one on, which he did, greatly improving the old saw, and a half hour's work on it with a file made a new saw. All forenoon the axe and the saw stood ready for the spending of surplus energy and the woodpile grew to such a size that it appeared as though we intended staying another month instead of another week.

Everybody works cutting wood, cleaning up camp, etc.

After the routine of the city with its lack of exercise, it is a treat to swing a keen axe or work rhythmically to the r-r - z-z of a crosscut saw as it eats its way through a healthy birch. Then again, there is a heap of satisfaction in looking at a neatly piled woodpile that you yourself have produced.

When Ray finished cleaning up the tent and around the fireplace and tables, it wouldn't possibly do to let a chip fly over in that direction. The camp was shipshape in every particular—we had everything that could be desired.

After dinner Bob and Ray decided to go to the station and Harve and Jess to try a little fishing in Salmon. As Bob and Ray took the canoe, Harve and Jess used Elmer's old boat, both of them sitting in the stern, each with a paddle, the bow high and swinging. They looked like an old hooker from the West Indies, or as Jess called her—the good ship "Hesperus." At some stubbs [stumps] north of Mrs. Cobb's, they threw in their lines and had great fun trying to catch the thief that continuously stole their bait. Harve broke a tip of Ray's Greenhart rod in the excitement, and Jess nearly cracked a rib laughing at him. But whoever stole the bait was too foxy—or too trouty—to be caught.

Late in the afternoon they hiked it for Trout Pond—Trout Pond. There is a magnetism about that place, especially for Harve and Jess.

The name Trout Pond will always be associated with trout—big trout and lots of them, and even this day, when they did not even have a bite except from a sunfish or a chub, will not deaden that fond association because Trout Pond is in a class by itself. One need not go to British Columbia or Algonquin Park for a wild setting, for on this evening Harve and Jess experienced a superior satisfaction that they need go no farther.

As the sun settled in the west, the wildlife appeared. Splash! A beaver gave the alarm to its mates; then the lake was still for a few moments until splash again as the beaver came to the surface a few hundred feet away. Then, seeming to realize that no harm would come to them, several of them came out, swimming back and forth between a small

Jess going after 'em. On his way to Trout Pond.

bay of lily pads and their house. They were probably laying in a supply of roots for the winter. Then to the left of the boat, three deer appeared in a small marsh (with the low setting sun full upon them) and came out to the water's edge to drink only a short distance from the boat. A doe, a fawn and what might have been a yearling. They were in no hurry. The doe was the first to feel alarmed and threw up her head, then jumped a few feet back into the bushes, the fawn following. There they stood watching Harve and Jess in the boat, while the third deer, with no apparent alarm, drank his fill, and then the three disappeared into the woods. A beaver splashed again, his great flat tail resounding as it struck the water. A couple of ducks swam out of a little bay and around a point out of sight near the Burnt Lake trail. From somewhere came the faint call of a loon.

The sun dropped behind the mountains and the evening chill reminded Harve and Jess that it was time to get back to camp. Going up the trail just passing the tote road, there was a big splash in the stream which, for the moment, made them think it was a beaver, but they were surprised to see a large buck leap from the stream and run through the bushes up the other shore. There he stopped and snorted. Harve and Jess went carefully down to the stream's edge and waited for a second look at a white tail as he bounded away, but the buck was too wise for that, and they went on and were soon on Salmon Lake again. The sun had long set, and the good old lake reflected the panorama of its beautiful shores in the perfectly quiet waters of the evening. As darkness settled, the mournful call of the loon floated across the lake—mournful, mysterious and weird, yet perfectly in harmony with all the surroundings and fitting perfectly into the setting of the evening, impressing one of its solitude. Again it came—first, a sort of tremolo, then a loon's smooth high call in its own weird key. Back at camp, Bob and Ray had supper all prepared. They had been to the station and brought back some bread, some candy and a daily paper, etc. On the way in, they saw a deer and some partridges.

The outside world didn't trouble us at all. We were to be in here another week, so why worry? Again in our blankets, the last sound before going to sleep was the plaintive call of the loon.

"H" [Harve]

Keeping the Sabbath Day in camp. Harve said it was the worst scrape he ever got into.

Sunday, August 24th

"Sunday, the day of rest." After a leisurely breakfast, including the usual pan-full of crispy fried brook trout, the bunch busied themselves with the occupations proper for the Sabbath Day in a well regulated camp—not Divine service (much as it was missed), but with other duties equally as godly if we believe that "Cleanliness is next to Godliness." Tidying up camp, washing of shirts, socks and underwear, to say nothing of the scrubbing and shaving of ourselves, kept everyone fully occupied for a couple of hours.

About 11:00, Bob and Ray took the canoe and decided to slip down to Trout Pond "just for a few." Starting out, Bob rigged up an archer trolling rig, thinking perhaps to connect with a "sammin," although knowing that few of these are caught in August. But luck was with him, and about half way down the lake, trolling in deep water, he had a strike, and from the way the rod tip bent and jerked, it was a good one. Meanwhile, thunder rumblings in the north gave warning of a storm approaching, but storm or no storm, no chances could be taken of losing that trout, and while Ray kept the canoe under bare headway, Bob proceeded to tire out Mr. Laker, which he successfully did, and in about fifteen minutes a beautiful specimen 17" long was in the net. It was then up to them to save themselves a soaking, to make Cobbs' campsite in quick time, which they did, and got under the old canvas there just as the first big drops started. Then, for a full half hour the lightning snapped and crackled and the thunder boomed while the rain came down in torrents. Then back to camp, where they found Jess and Harve putting the finishing touches on a fireside seat, backrest and all.

After a noonday lunch, a loaf and a smoke, the whole bunch set out for Trout Pond, Harve and Jess to do some photographing and Bob and Ray still with the idea of getting "just a few." The "few" were forthcoming and five nice trout were added to the larder, while Jess and Harve paddled around the pond disturbing the busy beaver. Back to camp at dusk, a good feed, a smoke before the fire and with the birch night logs piled on three deep, the bunch hit the boughs— another full day shot and shot right.

"R" [Ray]

Left to right: Harve, Ray, Jess and Bob.

Monday, August 25th

The bunch woke up, except Jess, about 6:30 to the sound of rain on the tent. It only lasted a few minutes, however, so we all turned out at 7 a.m. Jess started the oatmeal, Harve the coffee and Bob the trout, while Ray tended the fires and got the table in shape. The sun finally came out and things looked very good. We all took our time, and after doing all the little things about camp we could think of, Harve proceeded to take some pictures of Klim[6] in the making.

We then decided that we should have at least fifty dollars from the Merrel Soule Company if the pictures came out as they should and were accompanied by a good letter. (Any one of the bunch would write any kind of letter for fifty dollars.)

We then got out the topographic map and looked over the country to see where to go for an afternoon hike. Bob heard some stories (now known to be lies) about the wonderful fishing in the first Beech Ridge pond, so it was decided to go over there. At 11:45 we started up to

[6] Klim was powdered milk manufactured by Merrel Soule and later by the Borden Company.

Hawk Lake, around the south end of it, and when we reached the outlet there was some question as to just which way was the shortest to the old tote road. We got out the map and compass, and at Ray's suggestion took a due west course and run into the worst bunch of witchhopple we ever saw. Harve was for changing the course to the left; Bob was for the right in order to hit the old Totten & Crossfield Line, but in a few minutes we hit the tote road and followed it on to the head of Dismal Pond. There Bob found some of his old marks made five and six years ago. We then followed the tote road on up the Beech Ridge, and about halfway up Bob shot a hedge-hog [porcupine] with the .22. Harve then told how fine hedge-hog was when properly cooked, so we partly skinned the hog and took some of the meat, also the left hind foot for luck, which Harve wanted for his friend Pepper at Albany.

About this time, we heard thunder in the west, and each fellow said the same thing simultaneously. We went on and came to the Pond at 2:30. The country at this point was at one time lumbered of the soft wood and is now growing up in the thickest bunch of birch we ever saw. There are some beaver on the pond and they have a small house on the west side.

After sizing up the situation, it was decided to build a raft, so we looked for a dead tamarack and shortly found one. It was promptly cut down, but it wasn't enough for a good raft so we found a dead spruce nearby and cut that.

When it began to fall, it lodged in another tree and we had to cut that also. About this time, the usual afternoon rain cut loose, and

Cutting the tamarack for a raft.

oh, boy!—how it did come down. Bob and Harve built up a big fire, and Ray and Jess put the raft together which, by the way, was a daisy.

Ray then went out to try his luck, but those fellows who told such wonderful tales about the big trout in large numbers in the Beech Ridge Pond do great violence to the truth. While Ray was out on the raft, Harve took some pictures, as it had stopped raining, and Jess and Bob went on over to Darrow's old camp site, which was only a few minutes' walk.

This camp has all been destroyed, having been burned. The birch and wild cherry are growing up all over the old place. About this time, the rain cut loose again and this time we got soaked to the hide.

Jess and Bob went back to the pond where Ray was still trying it. It was 5:00 p.m. by this time, so we decided to start back. The bushes were all full of water and so was the old tote road. We came back to a point where Darrow had a trail to Willys Lake and decided to take that, but we had not gone 500 feet when we lost it. It was thought best to come back to Dismal and let Bob follow his old markings to Hawk Pond, and then if we got lost there would be someone to blame it on. But the blazes were fairly good and no trouble was experienced in

The completed raft.

reaching Hawk Pond. Just as we struck the pond, we jumped a big buck. Also, we startled a number of ducks on the pond. We went around to the north of the pond and hit the home trail, which looked very good, and then started down the mountain for camp, reaching there at 7:30 awfully wet.

We immediately changed our clothes, built up a real fire and at 8:30 had a big feed of creamed onions, mashed potatoes, tea, bread and butter, jelly and milk. We turned in at just 9:45 and just as we were rolling up in the blankets, the rain came down again, but we only gave it the laugh, and in less time than it takes to tell it, Jess was sawing right through a lot of hemlock knots.

"B" [Bob]

Tuesday, August 26th

This was the day we were supposed to have gone on the big hike to High Falls on the Oswegatchie, but when we woke up in the morning it was plainly to be seen that the weather had no intentions at all of clearing up. If we would but admit it, the unanimous thought at that time was very likely the same as Jess's, for as Jess put it, "When I heard

Fooling around camp.

that rain on the tent I said to myself 'By Gol, that's good—we don't have to go to High Falls today,'" and by the way, we all pounded our ear until after nine; that must have been the general feeling. We did manage to get rested, though, and had a very fine breakfast at about dinner time, which would be an awful disgrace in the woods if the weather had shown any decency. After breakfast, we just fooled around camp. Took a few pictures and cut some more wood between showers. Harve started a little candle factory and made seven candles from the grease from the burnt candles. He used the neck of a quart whiskey bottle for a mould.

Harve making candles.

Late in the afternoon we had dinner. Harve made a fine stew out of the hedge-hog meat, that is; Bob and Harve said it was fine. Ray and Jess acted a little queer about it as though they couldn't understand how anyone could eat the stuff. Harve and Bob both agreed that it was great stuff and couldn't understand why they were not eating more than they were. Bob called it "Sauer Brauten," but Jess corrected him to "Sour and Rotten." Harve offered Jess a piece of choice meat from the stew when he was chopping wood, but Jess only said "No, not now." After our late dinner, we all went to Trout Pond, going to the foot of Salmon in the canoe. Bob fished down the outlet of Salmon and got eight trout. Ray and Jess fished in Trout Pond and Darrow's boat and got four nice trout about 8 inches. Harve had the .22 and went after meat. He got one squirrel and another hedge-hog, but this time instead of only cutting enough meat off for a sample, he went at it right and took all there was, looking forward to a regular man's size portion of a most wholesome and savory stew. He knew Bob would be right there to do his share. This second hedge-hog won for Bob and Harve the name of "The Hedgehog Eaters" from Jess. Harve cut the meat up that night and got the "Sauer Brauten" started over the evening fire.

We had a fine supper of mashed potatoes, rice, tea, bread and jam—one of the few meals that we ate no trout. After we dried our clothes at the evening fire, we turned in, hoping that the morning might possibly be bright enough for an early start for High Falls and famous fishing.

"H" [Harve]

Mapping out the trip to High Falls.

Wednesday, August 27th

The camp awoke to the same weather conditions, and again the High Falls trip was delayed. One good feature about this rainy season is that everybody enjoys the sleep in the morning. After a late breakfast of oatmeal, toast, trout and coffee, Ray and Jess went to the station after more bread and sugar.

Ray and Jess start for Beaver River Station for bread, sugar and mail.

They fished the outlet on the way out, and the number caught was eleven. Showers of rain all day, so it made very little difference to Ray who fell in the creek. Harvey and Bob stayed in camp, and besides a fresh supply of balsam on the bed, a lot of wood was cut and things generally improved around the camp. All this energy was obtained from the Hedge-hog Stew Harvey made. Ray and Jess, on their return from the Settlement, were very hungry, but could not be induced to eat the stew Bob and Harvey claimed so much for. All hands did eat heartily of a good cornbeef hash and cornstarch pudding. Plenty of bread and sugar in camp now and all we want now is fair weather for the High Falls hike. It is raining at this writing.

But the fire burns in the fireplace before the tent and soon we will all be rolled in our blankets and the first man to awake will report on the weather. Rain or shine, we are having a good time and no doubt before the end of the week we will be able to write the report on fishing at High Falls.

"J" [Jess]

Right: Jess finishes up his entry in the log.

Below: Relaxing by the fire.

Thursday, August 28th

In spite of weather not too promising, the bunch got away to a late start, about eleven, bound for High Falls—all curious to learn what conditions they would find there, and going prepared for anything they might find. Two pack baskets, each about 40 lbs., two fish baskets, rods and the .22 made up the outfit.

Going up the inlet the canoe, with its 800 lb. load, grounded in the shallow water and Harve and Ray stepped overboard to help the craft along into deeper water, alternating with the packs. Good time was made—stopping for rest occasionally and once for a photograph of the bunch looking at a peculiar formation growing on a birch tree.

Clear Lake was crossed in the flat boat from the South Shore of Clear Lake.

Above: Jess, "Well, what shall we have for breakfast?" Below: (Left to right) Ray, Bob and Harve observe the burl in a yellow birch tree between Witchhopple and Clear Lakes.

(Left to right) Jess, Ray and Bob at the South Shore of Clear Lake.
Below: (Left to right) Ray, Bob and Jess. Lunch at East Pond, August 28th.

Then, Summit Pond and Big Crooked Lake skirted, and with the trail becoming more indistinct and full of windfalls, East Pond was reached about 1:30 p.m. Here a good lunch of bread and butter, beans, oranges and cookies fortified everyone for the long pull of the afternoon.

Crossing Robinson River in about an hour along a poor trail brought us to Toad Pond, where the bunch rested and Bob went down to the river and fished for a few minutes.

The river at this point certainly looks most "trouty," and one or another of us for some years has wet a line there, but always with the same results—no trout. However, rumor has it that a big mess of beautiful trout was once taken from this same spot, but you can't fry rumors. Downhill now and easier going, with a glimpse of the sliding falls of Robinson River, through the trees and soon the old Fur, Fin and Feather Camp appeared in sight through the big pines and spruces.

Ray and Bob inspect the remains of the Fur, Fin and Feather Camp.

But now, what only a few years ago was a snug log camp, was a tumbled-down ruin. With the steep side of Partlow Mountain ahead, some time was spent looking around among the debris of the old camp and poking about among the rusted and broken possessions of former occupants, and Bob, always the fisherman, went over to the river but with the same result as at Toad Pond. For some reason or other, the trout simply are not there in August. Now for the last lap—the stiff climb up Partlow Mountain and the long gradual descent on the opposite side, then the county line and the end of green timber. Fifteen minutes through the slash and we stood on the rocks beside the swift sliding waters above the falls.

*High Falls,
Cranberry
Lake Inlet.*

And there a surprise met our eyes; instead of the deserted place we had rather expected to find, knowing that the State had taken over this land some two years before, we saw a half dozen men moving about among the buildings—then two women dressed for the woods. Supper was being prepared over two or three different fires, and soon fishermen started dropping in, until, as we afterwards counted up, there were about twenty inhabitants scattered about among the half dozen buildings large and small, comprising, as we found, some four or five different parties. Five of the men were government surveyors with whom we had a pleasant visit about topographical maps completed and uncompleted.

After looking over the whole layout and finding one shack unoccupied, the gang threw down their packs and proceeded to make it habitable for the night. A good supply of balsam boughs lopped off and spread about made a bed that might easily have been worse. A few boards on a stump before the shack made a table, and inside of thirty minutes the gang was stowing away a good meal of hot tea, beans, bread and butter, marmalade and fried bacon. Meanwhile, Bob and Ray were trying the fishing in the big pool below the falls—famous for its big trout—but no trout rewarded their efforts, which was not to be wondered at when we considered the whipping that pool received daily at the hands of the fishermen camped there. However, to say "no trout" is not exactly true, for Bob did catch one which, after considerable stretching, was made to measure six inches—some trout! After night-fall, gathered before the shack about a nice fire, drying socks and telling stories, passed the hour until bedtime. Harve recorded the time and place by flashlight, and the attempt of another party to make a similar photograph of themselves created some diversion, inasmuch as they neglected to remove the cap from the flash cartridge we gave them, with the result that same went off with quite a startling pop.

Tired after the big day, the gang hit the boughs; that is, three of them did. Harve, however, hit the floor and pounding on the bare boards demanded if that was all the bed he got after him cutting the tree down too. Everybody hunched over and finally pacified him, and looking up at the tight roof with the stars shining through the cracks, everyone prayed for the good Lord to send no rain that night.

"R" [Ray]

Left to right: Ray, Jess, Bob and Harve, by flashlight at High Falls Camp.

Friday, August 29th

Prayers were not answered last night, or else the Lord left somebody else on the job, for shortly after midnight we were awakened by the gentle raindrops on the roof of the shack. There was some argument as to who had the rubber blanket, but it was finally dug out from between Jess and Bob and put over the bunch. The rain continued to come through the roof for some time, but by carefully manipulating the rubber, the water was shunted off the bed. About this time, Harve discovered that some water had gotten in one of the packs and wet his camera—we will omit his language.

The rain at last let up, and the next thing we knew it was 7 a.m. and a beautiful morning. We turned out and in a few minutes had a good breakfast of bacon, pancakes, jelly and coffee.

We visited a little more with some of the other campers and guides and then decided to hit for the county line and there decide on the itinerary for the day. We reached the line in about fifteen minutes and spent about a half hour in trying to decide on what to do. As the grub was low and there was some question about getting enough trout to eat, we decided to push on over Partlow Mountain to Fur, Fin and Feather, and possibly go from there to the Five Ponds. It was a long, hard pull over the mountain, and when we finally reached F.F. & F. Bob fished the river for over a half hour with no success. It was nearly noon then, and after some argument

Bob, Ray and Harve after breakfast.

*Ray and Bob
at the north
end of
Clear Lake.*

as to when and where we should lunch, Jess took a very decided stand to have [it] there and then, so we did. We collected all the bottles, pieces of glass and breakable stuff and set them up on the various trees and branches and shot them to pieces with the .22. A little after one o'clock, we started out very strong and made Toad Pond in 40 minutes. Here we stopped to try the fishing in the outlet, but with no success. We then came along in very fair trim, stopping only three times to change packs until we reached Clear Lake, where we found the boat as we left it.

We all piled in with Harve on the oars, and in fifteen minutes were on the south shore landing. We stopped at Mud, and Ray and Bob took the boat and went out to the spring hole in the middle. They connected with an 8" trout but that was all. All kinds of trout could be seen in the spring hole, but they could not be induced to bite. Then they drove them off just to see them scatter.

At just 6 p.m. we left Mud and came on down past Witchhopple to the landing and hit camp at 7:30. We all agreed once more that Salmon Lake had it on all of them. Harve got busy with one of his good feeds and we sure had a regular meal. We figured that day the rainy weather was over, as we had had one fine day. But—just before we turned in it began to leak again and we all went to sleep listening to the rain on the tent.

In our absence someone visited our camp and left us six doughnuts and some cookies. We don't know who they were, but we thank them.

"B" [Bob]

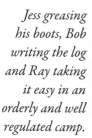

Jess greasing his boots, Bob writing the log and Ray taking it easy in an orderly and well regulated camp.

Saturday, August 30th

After yesterday's trip, all stuck to their blankets until late. The morning broke clear, and outside of a lot of shooting and wood cutting, the forenoon was spent in putting the camp in order.

Bob and Ray tried for a lake trout while Harvey and Jess took pictures, but the rain started again and soon all were snug in the tent with the ever-cheerful log fire in front. The camp talk now often refers to the morrow, when we will have to pack and tear down the tent. It usually is short, as it is a subject not very well liked by any. Harvey and Jess would like to photograph some of the beautiful effects seen on the Salmon Lake in the late evening, but those are scenes the campers will have to cherish in their memories and talk about while visiting one another in their city homes.

Sunday, August 31st—Last day of fishing

After a wonderful night's rest the bunch woke up at 7 a.m. with rain on the tent. We all lay there and talked things over and made plans for another year. A little after 8 o'clock Ray got up and kicked the big fire together, which was still burning, having been replenished in the night. He also built a fire in the stove. Then Bob turned out, and in a short time after him Harve poked his head out of the tent and remarked that it looked like an all-day rain, but he didn't care. Then Jess gave an extra snort and piled out. The rain seemed to come a little harder all the time, but we managed to get a real he-man breakfast of prunes, bacon, oatmeal, fried potatoes, coffee and cakes.

Shortly after breakfast, which was about 9:30, the rain cut loose for fair and oh, boy! She came across the lake in sheets. About 11 it slackened and the mists began to roll away, so the packs were gotten out and we all got real busy so that by 1 o'clock everything was packed in the four packs and two rolls. Then Ray, Harve and Jess took the canoe and started down the lake, leaving Bob at the camp to do the last cleaning up so as to show the next people who might happen along that four regular guys had been there.

Top: Jess and Harve. No smiles left.
Bottom: (Left to right) Harve, Jess, Ray and Bob. Last night in camp.

All of the remaining stuff, including a goodly supply of wood, was left in apple-pie order. By that time, Ray was back with the canoe and then he and Bob took down the tent and rolled it up in the canvas bag and loaded the balance of the duffel in the canoe, leaving the place at 2:25 p.m.

At the foot of the lake they met Harve and Jess who had just returned from the tote road, where they had taken two of the packs. Then the four took the canoe and the balance of the duffel to Trout Pond. The loads were heavy and did not carry as easily as they did going in. At Trout Pond, Ray and Jess took the canoe and started for Big Burnt and the river via Dave Conkey's old camp, on directions given by Bob. Harve and Bob went back to the tote road, where they packed up the heavy packs and started for the river, getting there at 6 p.m. After a wait of two hours, Ray and Jess showed up and proceeded to bawl out Bob on account of the directions he had given for getting from Conkey's old camp to the river. Bob finally admitted that he had never been over the trail, but had some hear-say directions which he said Sam Mills had given him. Ray and Jess agreed that either Sam Mills or Bob was a liar, or perhaps both, but finally convinced Bob that the trail was bum and ended in a swamp.

It was just 8 o'clock then, so the bunch had a good feed and left the river just as it was getting dark. They arrived at Beaver Station at just 9:10 P.M, and after a good visit with Pop and Deliah, left at 10:06 for Utica. Arrived at Utica about 1 a.m., and Harve took [the] trolley, and Ray, Jess and Bob took the Main Line at 2:15, arriving at Syracuse at 3:20 a.m. Before parting at Utica, it was agreed that this was the best vacation ever, and it was further agreed to get together again in 1920.

"B" [Bob]

Chapter 12

Spring Fishing in the Adirondacks

The Reverend A. L. Byron-Curtiss with his prized catch of thirty-five trout hanging in front of his Nat Foster Lodge on North Lake.

THE LURE OF SPRING FISHING for brook trout is a powerful enticement to those who have experienced the first rises after the ice departs from a trouty Adirondack lake. The itch begins subtly, sometimes as early as the first February thaw, but spreads swiftly as soon as four or five sunny, late-winter days arrive consecutively, drawing the sweet sap of the sugar maple to their tender new buds or to a syrup maker's spiles. It is a primitive draw, not unlike a pilgrimage, a journey repeated season after season since long before words were used to attempt its description.

To one afflicted by the itch, there is only one thing to do. Go fishing!

As agreed the previous fall, Bob teamed up with Ray Dunham for a trip to the Adirondacks in late spring 1920. Their destination was North Lake, to take advantage of an open invitation offered by Ray's old friend the Rev. A. L. Byron-Curtiss. The headwaters of the Black River had served up the kind of sporting adventure that Ray appreciated and he hoped it would again satisfy everyone's itch to catch fish.

With Byron-Curtiss as their seasoned guide, the fishing lived up to its promise. An entry in the Nat Foster Lodge log book reveals the day's events.

> May 29, 1920: Dunham and Gillespie arrived. A day of extraordinary luck fishing. Occupants, feeling venturesome, went to Hardscrabble Lake. Joe and B-C[7] with crippled fishing outfits. Joe with a short line and B-C with a rod without a tip, yet a splendid mess of trout. Forty-five—each weighing one half pound. Ideal day for [fishing] Hardscrabble—ripples on the water and not too bright a day.

B-C had not recorded it, but their dinner no doubt included a few "brookies" sizzling over the camp stove, possibly complemented by a few bottles of the minister's own home brew. Ever since Congress had passed Prohibition the previous fall, the locally crafted "mountain dew" was the best around.

With bellies full and a glowing campfire, Bob and Ray might have been witness to B-C's recounting of a rip-snorting tale invented by a member of the local Liars' Club, or they might have heard about the misadventures of the North Lake Navy, of which Byron-Curtiss was "Commodore."

Whichever stories were told, the tingle from a mug full of "mountain dew" helped the laughter flow, a chatter that echoed across the lake and disappeared above the dim reflection of Ice Cave Mountain.

---

[7] B-C is how The Rev. A. L. Byron-Curtiss referred to himself in his camp journal. Joseph was his son.

Chapter 13
Work!

*Alexander Graham Bell on his telephone
in New York calling Chicago in 1892.*

I N THE FALL OF 1920, Bob was offered an opportunity that, if he
accepted, would curtail his Adirondack activities for several years.
The growing popularity of the telephone had created a worldwide
demand for installations and with it a demand for people like Bob with
expertise installing the necessary infrastructure. When the International
arm of Western Electric was awarded the contract to lay the first big
trunk cables in Sweden, they invited Bob to supervise the installation.
It meant leaving his family or moving them overseas, but in either case,
it was too great an opportunity to pass up.

On November 7, 1920, the *Elmira Telegram* ran this short news item
about Bob's new position:

Elmiran in Charge

Will Supervise Construction of Cable from Sweden to Holland.
The Western Electric Company has placed a former Elmiran, Robert
Gillespie, in charge of the construction of a large cable which is to be
built from Stockholm, Sweden to Guttenberg, Holland, a distance
of 400 miles. The work will take a year.

Mr. Gillespie will be remembered as an employee of the American
Telephone and Telegraph Company in various capacities, and was
stationed at Albany until the recent appointment. His family will
return to Syracuse while Mr. Gillespie is in Europe.

The predicted length of the job was overly optimistic. It lasted more
than two years, so Bob brought his family over for an extended visit.

While Bob was in Sweden, Harve Dunham was honing his skills in
the trade of commercial art and Ray was in Akron, Ohio, working for
the B. F. Goodrich Tire Company. During his career, Harve worked in
New York City, Albany, Washington and Baltimore before finally settling down in Utica and working at the Mohawk Engraving Company.
Ray ended up back in Central New York too, in Syracuse with his wife
and their two daughters.

Up at North Lake, Byron-Curtiss's camp log book mentioned one
more Dunham trip while Bob was overseas. Ray Dunham, in the company of E. Stuart Mills, arrived at North Lake on May 13, 1922. Their
host warned them there had been "no particular fishing" in the lake
or river so far, but they laid aside the doubtful conditions and hiked
to Grindstone Creek thinking stream fishing might yield some luck.
But the prediction held true. They "did not get even a nibble." As a
side trip, they ventured to an abandoned lumber camp and salvaged a
few useful items to bring back: "a metal water pail, one metal bushel
basket that can be used as a wash tub, a double-bitted ax, a file, some
nails, and a stove lid lifter."

When they returned to camp the out-of-luck anglers offered to help with a "sundry of odd jobs." On May 14, 1922, Byron-Curtiss recorded this brief entry.

> Fourth Sunday after Easter. Prayers said in camp at 10 a.m. As fishing has proven to be poor so far, and an opportunity of going out in p.m. is to be had with Raymond Dunham and his friend in his Essex car, B-C embraced the opportunity to go and started at 3 p.m. Weather: pleasant.

The worst fishing that Byron-Curtiss ever experienced in spring may have foreshadowed some trouble ahead in summer. A fate similar to what befell Elmer Wilder and Camp Happy appeared to be on the horizon for Byron-Curtiss's beloved Nat Foster Lodge. Like Elmer, Byron-Curtiss had been informed by the state that his camp was on state land, but unlike Elmer, who knew he had no claim to the property, Byron-Curtiss had fought tenaciously to keep his. He believed in his claim of ownership and was willing to try any legal argument to try to keep the camp.

Top: The interior of the old Nat Foster Lodge. Below: The lodge after it was rebuilt.

In the end, all the litigation accomplished was to forestall the inevitable and to eke out a few more precious seasons at the North Lake camp.

Three weeks after Bob and Ray had escorted The Reverend down the bumpy North Lake Road to catch a train at the Forestport Station, Ranger E. W. Blue broke into the unoccupied camp on June 6, 1922, as ordered, moved all the furnishings of any value to the woodshed and proceeded to tear the camp down. At least Elmer knew it was coming. Byron-Curtiss was not so lucky.

Angry and dejected, he jotted these few lines (referring to himself in the third person) in the camp log book when he recovered it from the woodshed.

Little did B-C think when he closed camp on May 14th that it would be the last time he was to see his old Nat Foster Lodge. But on June 6, rangers from the Conservation Commission tore down the dear old shanty because foresooth, it is on the Forest Preserve. B-C was told of operations by telephone, by his good friend Charlie Brown, on the day of the rape and today B-C came in accompanied by Arthur Griffiths of Willard and reviewed the wreck. The boat house and wood house are left standing and the furniture stands therein. Drs. Jones and Fuller very kindly letting us use their camp; we are comfortably honored therein. B-C feels rather blue over the loss of his summer retreat, where he had over twenty happy summers—five of the summers spent here entirely.

Byron-Curtiss had lost his camp, but not his friends and neighbors. Within a month, those friends and neighbors made sure B-C got a new lot with a clear title. With their help, what was left of Nat Foster Lodge had been salvaged and everyone assembled for a good old-fashioned camp rising.

Nat Foster Lodge was built anew, better than ever.

Chapter 14
West Canada Creek

The Third Trip Journal of Bob Gillespie
with Zene Gillespie, Harve Dunham,
Ray Dunham, Doc Eastman and Fritz Neu
August 17, 1924–September 1, 1924

THE FINAL JOURNAL OF BOB AND HIS FRIENDS documents a two-week adventure to West Canada Creek in August 1924. It begins on a rainy summer night.

Sunday, August 17, 1924.

It was midnight of August 16th or rather the first hour of the 17th, depending on whether it was Eastern Standard or Daylight time. We had just set the alarm clock for 4:30 a.m. and figured on an early start from Utica. All signs pointed to rainy weather for it was raining very hard when we went to bed. We had loaded all the duffel in Harve's car. It seemed but a few minutes after we said Good Night when the alarm sounded. Oh: what a vast difference between the alarm that wakes one up to go fishing and the one that calls you to work.

We were dressed, washed and ready to start in fifteen minutes. Oh, but wasn't it raining! We weren't bothered with traffic on Genesee Street, however. After a good breakfast at the Richmond Lunch, we left the city in a driving rain.

Right: Harve never let a little mud get in the way of a day in the woods.

Bottom: Hinckley Reservoir on a rainy day.

It was good daylight when we reached Barneveld and, by the time we reached Hinckley, the rain had practically let up. It was one of those mornings, however, when anybody's guess on the weather for the day was good and the guesses were all the way from a downpour to bright sunshine.

Map of West Canada Creek,
Nobleboro to West Canada Lakes

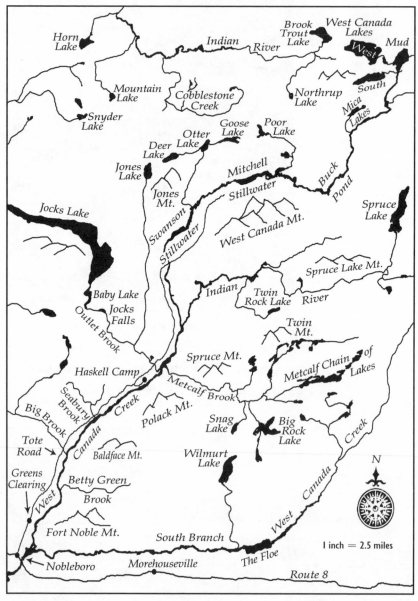

Horn
Lake

Indian
River

Brook
Trout
Lake

West Canada
Lakes

West
Mud

Mountain
Lake

Cobblestone
Creek

Northrup
Lake

South

Snyder
Lake

Mica
Lakes

Otter
Lake

Goose
Lake

Poor
Lake

Deer
Lake

Jones
Lake

Mitchell

Jones
Mt.

Stillwater

Buck
Pond

Swanson

Jocks Lake

Stillwater

West Canada Mt.

Spruce
Lake

Spruce Lake Mt.

Baby Lake

Indian

Twin
Rock Lake

River

Jocks
Falls

Twin
Mt.

Outlet Brook

Spruce Mt.

Metcalf Chain of
Lakes

Haskell Camp

Metcalf Brook

Seabury
Brook

Big Brook

Canada
Creek

Polack Mt.

Snag
Lake

Big
Rock
Lake

Creek

Tote
Road

Baldface Mt.

Wilmurt
Lake

West Canada

Greens
Clearing

Betty Green

West

Brook

N

Fort Noble Mt.

South Branch

I inch = 2.5 miles

Nobleboro

Morehouseville

The Floe

Route 8

From Noboleboro to West Lake is 18 miles.

Dan Clemmons's Place.

We came around the north side of the Reservoir on a very rough road and on past Willie Leight's old place, finally reached Dan Clemmons's house which was the old Shufelt place.

We had made arrangements with Dan to haul our stuff to Camp, Dan allowed as to how it was a little moist and the road would be full of water but he guessed he could make it.

Dan Clemmons crossing Big Brook with his wagon.

The remains of the old dam at Nobleboro. Fort Noble Mt. in the distance.

He had a good woods wagon and a fine team, a grey and a dark bay. After the usual preliminaries of getting acquainted and comparing notes, we transferred the duffel to Dan's wagon and put the car in the barn.

Dan said it was eleven miles to Trume's Camp.[8] We jogged along in good shape until we reached Nobleboro as the road was fine. From there to a point where the tote road breaks off the old Jock's Lake Road, is a very fair woods road. We all rode up to this point but after the tote road was reached no one but a good teamster who was used to the road could stay in the wagon.

The three of us took the trail which follows close to the creek for some little ways and the tote road is back in the woods.

About a mile from the Jock's Lake road up the creek is the first still water on an old log driving dam. There are two old log camps here and an old fellow by the name of Peachy Barse makes one of these camps his home. Peachy is a man about 70 years old and it is safe to say that he hasn't had a bath all over for 69 years. The camp, his clothes, himself and the ground in front are all the same color, viz., a dirty brown.

8 Trume Haskell owned the camp that the men rented for the trip.

Left to right: Ray, Peachy Barse and Harve on Peachy's porch.

Peachy had a little garden which we all admired and he told us to help ourselves to some of his beans. Harve picked about 2 quarts and we gave Peachy a quarter which he assured us he didn't want but which went into his pocket before he said a word.

He finally wished us good luck, said goodbye and ended up by telling us if we had any grub left that we could leave it with him on the way out.

Arriving at camp. Left to right: Ray, Bob and Dan Clemmons.

Looking upstream, the creek was low.

We finally reached camp at 1:10. Clemmons fed his team and it was only a few minutes before a good fire was built, the duffel unloaded and dinner was under way. A little after two we sat down to fried ham, boiled potatoes, bread, butter and coffee and topped it all off with some preserved plums.

Clemmons, in accordance with customary etiquette of his kind, promptly beat it after dinner.

We then proceeded to arrange our stuff and put the camp in right and proper shape. Harve, as usual, was very fussy about the grub and had to have it just so. We always let him have his way.

It's a long time from 4 a.m. to 6 p.m., especially when one has been on the move all the time and we were all a bit fagged when we had the last of our arrangements completed at 6 p.m.

However, after the rain is always a good time to try 'em and so we strung up the rods and went up the stream a few hundred feet. Harve and I had little or no success but Ray stuck it out until his worms were exhausted.

When he came into camp about dusk he had seven trout, the largest one being about 12" or ¾ lbs. He felt very proud over his performance and proceeded to tell Harve and me how good his was.

Harve and I got most of the supper and then, after washing up the dishes and making up the beds, we retired about 10:00 p.m., still arguing as to what kind of time we would keep in the woods.

R.M.G [Bob Gillespie]

Monday, August 18th.

Coming into the woods, opening up camp and getting things squared around made a long, hard day and we slept soundly. However, I claim that, no matter how soundly I am sleeping, I will wake up if any gosh hanged hedge hog comes within 44 ft. of my bed. Consequently along in the night some time, I woke up and heard a crunch, crunch, crunch, outside on the porch. He

First afternoon's catch by Ray.

beat it before we could get the artillery into action but I sure am going to shoot him dead and all his family too before I leave.

Good beds are not conducive to early rising and it was after seven o'clock, sensible time, when we kicked back the covers. Breakfast, including trout, was soon tucked beneath our belts and, while cleaning up the kitchen later, a bird flew through the door, straight across the room and crashed against the window glass so hard that Harvey picked him off the window sill. We identified it as a grosbeak—what kind we didn't know.

Harve and the grosbeak.

Left: A falls on Honnedaga Outlet Brook.

Bottom of facing page: Falls on Metcalf Brook.

For the day we decided to try our luck up the [Honnedaga] Outlet Brook. Fifteen minutes brought us there. About ¾ mile up the stream Bob dropped off then myself and Harve went on up as far as the falls before starting to fish. The trout ran rather small but we managed to get a fair mess. On the way back we stopped at the rifts in the main stream just above the camp and I picked up a couple there. Nightfall found us sitting down to a hearty supper not the least of which was hot Johnny cake. Then a few smokes, a trap set for Mr. Hedgehog and we hit the hay. 21 trout this day—none large enough to talk about.

R. F. D [Ray Dunham]

Tuesday, August 19th.

To start this day very early which was somewhere along the small hours of the morning, I woke up to the gnawing of Mr. Hedgehog chewing underneath the porch flooring. The 22 was loaded and I leaned out of the window and let 2 shots go through the flooring. A moment later I heard him go lumbering through the bushes toward the stream. I was well awake by then and got up and went out onto the porch. The hedgehog had disappeared. There was a thick mist or fog but I could see the trees across the stream. A half moon hung over the mountain and the light penetrated the fog just enough to give everything a strangely artificial appearance. The woodpile and the bushes near the camp seemed to be painted in a grayish or bluish monotone. A rabbit thumped and jumped away and all was still except the never-ceasing song of the waters of the West Creek. I went back to bed feeling thankful to the hedgehog who had given me the opportunity to look out on the creek at this secret hour. It was not long before daylight. When I got up for the day the mists were rolling up the mountainside and the dew was dripping off the porch roof.

We had no trip planned. During the forenoon we stayed around camp and nothing of importance happened except a pudding was made. We were growing a little anxious for the trail, the camp life with its soft warm beds and its oversized meals was making us logy. Whether this was imagination or not, in the afternoon Raymond and I climbed the mountain east of the camp and Bob took a hike up Metcalf Creek. When Bob came back he reported nothing but 3" trout but a very pretty stream.

The trip up the mountain was very interesting. We picked up a lumber road back of the old camp across the creek which we followed to where it crossed a rocky slide which went straight up the side of the mountain. It was as even as a pavement and covered with damp moss. Every hundred feet or so there would be a 4 or 5 ft. step or a crevasse or some places a mass of boulders. The slide averaged about 10 ft. across. We followed the slide nearly to the top by the aid of the trees along the side and fallen logs. Nearly anywhere to within a hundred feet of the top of the mountain there was good drinking water. A short distance from the top of the slide was a slash where we obtained a fine view of the country to the west of West Creek and north of the Swanson. We picked out Jones Mountain and West Canada Mountains and where Northrup Lake ought to lie. Patches of green timber stood out and also the bright patches of bare rock on the mountain back of the camp and on the mountain towards Jock's Lake. Trume's Camp and West Creek were just 1000 feet below. The mountain is less than a mile from the camp and it took about one hour to climb.

While we were eating supper, Bob's brother Zene from Pittsburg and Doc Eastman of Erie, Pa., came in. They had left Rome, N.Y., about 1:00 p.m. They were tired but we had plenty for them to eat and they proved that an all day auto ride and six miles of pack and trail gave a man an appetite and also an appreciation for a good bed and a night's rest.

—Harve

On the porch of Trume Haskell's camp. Left to right: Zene, Doc, Bob and Ray.

Wednesday, August 20th.

At just daybreak I rolled out and woke up the rest. Just as I got the fire well under way, Zene came downstairs. Then in a few minutes all hands showed up and Harve and I got the breakfast. It was a corker and enough for 20 men. How all hands did lay to it!

We had discussed the Northrup Lake trip a good deal but it was finally decided right after breakfast that we would all go. We cleaned the dishes up in a hurry and got the grub out and packed.

We were in quite a hurry but we managed to load the packs about evenly. We had 4 packs and Eastman carried a tump line.[9]

We left camp about 8:10 Standard Time. The day was a little cloudy but not too warm. The going was good. We struck up the creek over an old tote road that brought us to the Swanson Stillwater old dam. This was the first six miles of the trip. The Swanson is on the Adirondack League Club but we had a pass to cross their property. We ducked around the camp and took a side trail to the north about a half mile west of the Swanson. Just as we struck this trail it began to rain a little. We walked on up the trail which was a very good one until we came to a forks. After some little discussion we took the right hand one. We walked about 5 minutes and then discovered it went too far to the southeast. We then came back to the forks. Just about that time it began to rain quite a little. The trail was fine—all cut out and bridged. We walked along until about 1:30 when we stopped at a little stream for lunch. We had some cheese sandwiches.

After lunch we pushed on until about 3:00 p.m., when there was a flash and a crash and it began to rain very hard. We found two large rocks with a good hole under them and we crawled into them. It was good protection and we kept dry. Here we lost about an hour. After that we followed the trail on up the creek and finally came out at one of the League Camps on Otter Lake. We looked the Camp over and, while there, there was another downpour and some thunder and lightning. We seriously considered staying there over night but finally

[9] A tump line is a sling or strap slung over the forehead or chest to help carry a pack, packbasket or a bundle of blankets, etc.

decided to push on. There was no trail to the north of the lake so we followed through the woods and to the trail on the northeast side, then struck the trail to Goose Lake. It was a fair trail but in place of landing at the front of the lake we got on the old original trail to the north. It was beginning to rain again and also get late so we stopped on the north side of the lake and made camp. Gosh, but things were wet.

We soon had a good fire and then cut a big supply of spruce for the beds. We pitched the shelter tent and also a pup tent. Eastman had the pup tent and four of us the shelter tent.

When we unpacked the duffel we found that we had neglected to put in any plates, knives, forks, and spoons. Too much of a hurry to get away. However, each one of us had a few odd articles in his personal kit so we got along in good shape. The rain very kindly let up while we made camp and had supper but after supper it started again.

We turned in about 9:30 and, while it was a wet night, it was very warm and bed felt good. We were all very tired but with Northrup Lake only a few miles away we had visions of filling the pack with trout. It had been said that in Northrup if one puts on 3 hooks he will get three trout.

Making camp at Goose Lake.

Just about as we were falling off to sleep there was the damndest explosion or rifle shot near the camp. Some of us thought it a rifle and others thought it was an old cartridge in the fire. We accused Eastman of firing off his 22 rifle and sneaking back in the pup tent but he denied it and then we finally agreed that a .22 would not make that racket. Some of us thought there was some one coming up the lake in a boat and fired a high-power rifle. We discussed it at quite some length and finally went to sleep hearing queer noises in the woods and people walking. I woke up or half wakened in about an hour and saw two men going through the woods with a flashlight. They were walking away from camp.

But the mystery of the gun and explosion was not solved.

We were all dry in the little tent on a good bed of spruce and balsam and very tired.

Several times before midnight we would wake up and try to figure out the explosion and other queer things.

—Bob

Thursday, August 21st.

A fair morning and very welcome after all the rain of yesterday. We all passed a very comfortable night in spite of the disadvantages of making a wet camp last evening. A none too hearty breakfast was soon prepared and eaten with our makeshift tools and again we were on our way to Northrup Lake. Harvey took the packs on the Club boat he had found last evening and rowed to the head of Goose Lake where we met him. Shouldering our packs we set out over a very poor trail for Poor Lake. About halfway there we crossed the Club line and were again on State land. Poor Lake we reached without any trouble but there the trail ended. After much scouting around to pick up some sort of a trail around the north end of the lake, we decided that no trail existed. We then laid out our course by compass and map aiming to skirt around the shoulder of one mountain and go through a notch between two others to Northrup Lake—all of which sounds very simple but which in actual traveling calls for many pow-wows and much consulting of map and compass. However, we hit the notch and came upon water flowing north which could go nowhere else than into Northrup Lake. And, sure enough, we soon sighted water through the trees and one look showed us our destination had been reached. It was twelve-thirty and we were all more than glad that we had arrived at the object of our trip. Not far from the lake we noticed a large hemlock from which the bark had been removed . We all knew that this meant that somewhere we would find a bark leanto. We hoped to find it in good condition and we were not disappointed. Setting well above and overlooking the lake we found it—well built and tight, filled in at the sides with spruce boughs—a good fireplace in front—it sure was a welcome sight. We threw down our packs with a satisfied grunt and got busy. I went down to the lake to look around.

The shack on Northrup Lake. Left to right: Zene, Doc and Harve.

It is a pretty sheet of water about 2610 feet above sea level, about a third of a mile long and half as wide, shaped like a wedge. Its beauty is marred, as is that of so many lakes in the woods, by dead standing timber around the shores, the result of the raising of the water level

Breakfast at a Northrup Lake shanty.
Left to right: Harve, Ray, Bob and Zene.

by beaver. Two rafts were staked against the shore, one I judged large enough for three men and the other for two. Finding these meant the saving of an hour or two of hard work. Going back to the bark leanto I found lunch almost ready. Meager eats inside us we set out to get trout enough for a regular feed. Northrup Lake had been given a marvelous reputation and we hoped it would bear it out. It did apparently for first crack out of the box I was fast to a good one. He fought well and the whole trip was made worth while by that one trout. We caught ten in a couple of hours and then back to the camp where they were soon sizzling in the pan. I ate mine off a birch bark plate with a pocket knife to take it apart properly. Well, anyway, there certainly is one big advantage in not having any dishes—you don't have to wash them. After a smoke or two we were ready to hit the boughs. The leanto was ample for the five of us and the pack baskets as well. A half hour later, if any one had come near that camp, he would have heard a fine orchestra. Four good men played four different tunes with Harvey in the lead. He snores, as Doc says, both on the intake and the exhaust and wins by a big nose. Zene says he never snored in his life. I think he's a liar.

I am glad I had my map with me on this trip. Wish I might have had a chance to look at it. I tried often but no sooner would I have it opened up when some one would bellow out, "Lemme see your map, will yuh?" And I wouldn't hurt his feelings by telling him to go to hell for the world. Besides they were all in and I don't believe they had strength enough left to get out their own maps any way.

—*R.F.D. [Ray]*

The two rafts on Northrup Lake.

Top: Harve. Left: Harve and Doc.

Friday, August 22nd.

Some one was up prowling around as I raised my head to see what it was all about. The moon was shining brightly. There seemed to be no signs of morning. Doc Eastman was starting the fire. I pulled the blanket over my head and dozed off again. The next time I awoke I saw that the sky to the east showed signs of brightening and I got up and prepared what everyone agreed was a light breakfast but I knew just how much grub was in the camp and how many men were to eat it and how many meals there would be before we hit Trume's Camp again and also I knew that we had to eat strong on the day out.

After breakfast we went out on the rafts to see if the famous Northrup Lake would live up to her reputation. She had the night before, considering the short time we had fished. But today she fell short only yielding eighteen trout. They all were nice ones except two. The largest was about ¾ lb. I say nice—I mean just the best size for eating, about nine or ten inches long.

Zene was telling how he was at Trume Haskell's garage once when a couple of fellows drove up. Their appearance showed they had just come from a sojourn in the woods. He asked Trume if he wanted to see a mess of trout and opened a large creel which was filled with nice trout. "My Gawd but they are beauties," said Trume. "You've been up to Northrup Lake, haven't you boys?" The two fishermen were surprised and wanted to know at once how he knew. "Pink bellies," said Trume, "As soon as I saw them trout I knew they come from Northrup Lake by them pink bellies. But that is a fine mess." The fishermen replied that they could have had a pack basket full just as well as not.

I never saw trout fight so for their size as did the trout on Northrup and the sport I had with those few trout will always be remembered.

The fishing is certainly better in the spring of the year. As this was the last of August and the days were very bright, it is doubtful if better fishing could have been had under the same conditions on any lake in the Adirondacks.

Doc and Zene and I were sitting in the camp when Doc says, "Look, Ray's got one." The camp was high above the lake and through an opening in the trees we could see the raft where Bob and Ray were fishing. Ray was playing a good fish and Bob was ready with the net. The fish fought well with now and then a splash on the surface until at last he quieted down and Bob reached down and lifted him in the net. The lake through the trees, with the raft and two fisherman, was picturesque enough to have a real tang of wildness but, in addition to this, to watch them play and land that fish was a better composition than any motion picture setting I had ever seen.

We fished pretty well over the entire lake but all of our fish were caught on the upper end, that is, above the island.

We noticed and spoke of a gelatin-like growth in the lake, large masses of it in odd shapes and wondered if it had always been there or whether the beaver dams on the inlet and on the outlet of the lake itself, which had raised the lake several feet, had had any effect on the water to cause it to form. The lake had been raised so as to make quite an area of dead timber and dead warm water at the inlet end of the lake. A succession of beaver dams on any stream must make the water warmer in that stream. Trout may stand a certain amount of pollution in the water if the water is cold but if the water is warm they can not live.

Bob on a large yellow birch tree cut by beavers.

In the afternoon Bob and Zene went exploring for a better and easier way for us to start on our return trip and reported a direct route and easier traveling as far as the pug hole. It was agreed that those who knew the country better than we probably came in to Northrup by way of the Swanson and Mitchell Stillwaters on West Creek and then north through the woods. On our trip in we had seen many blazes which did not seem to lead anywhere. They may have been made for trap lines.

The trout finished out our evening meal. Doc gave us advice on eating too much fried food and proceeded to roast his trout in a novel way on a forked stick.

As we were just getting rolled up in our blankets we heard thunder and soon the rain came. It rained quite hard with an occasional clap of thunder and flash of lightning. The bark roof proved to be watertight and we drew in our feet and dozed off listening to the sputtering of the raindrops in the bed of hot coals in the fireplace.

—Harve

Saturday, August 23rd.

We were up a little after daybreak. Oh what a wet morning and patches of fog all over! It must have rained all night.

We deliberated a little as to whether or not to remain at Northrup another day but Eastman and Zene finally decided it so we began to pack up. The rain let up and as we had a big fire it wasn't so hard to get going. We loaded the packs as nearly even as we could and, after a good breakfast, we started at 7:10 a.m. We turned our backs to [the] lake and said Goodbye Northrup, most of us vowing we would see it again.

We started up through the gap but it was only a few minutes until the trail was lost. Zene and I tried to find our marks of the day before and after some back and forth business we finally found them and got down to what we thought was the pug hole [round puddle] on the map.

By this time we were all good and wet as the woods were soaked.

We held a council and, after comparing all the compasses and much argument we struck a course over the mountain. It was rough going and we stopped often to look at the map and compare notes. The natural inclination was to keep to the left as that kept us on one contour but the compass told us to go to the right. We were also afraid that, if we kept too far to the right, we would miss the head end of Poor Lake and then we would be up against it. The fog was so thick we could see but a short distance and the going was very rough.

After some little time we began to go downhill and finally came out on a slough or swamp. There was another big pow wow as to what it was but finally it was agreed that it must be the lower end of Poor Lake. We then pursued a northwest course and, in a few minutes, came out on open water which we knew was Poor Lake.

Ray said we certainly were a fine bunch to follow a compass and he would hate to see where we would come out if we had to run a line 5 miles long. Zene got a little excited and gave us a lecture on the compass, etc., but about that time the sun came out and then it was easy. We rested a while at the head of Poor Lake and then hit the trail to Goose. The trail was not the best but it was easy to follow and we were glad to feel that we did not have to depend on the compass. We came right along and hit Goose in a short time. We found the club boat near the upper end of the lake so loaded our stuff and ourselves in and rowed the boat. Just after we landed we saw a very beautiful deer. Also we saw several kinds of ducks on the lake. None of the game seemed to be at all shy. We struck Otter in a short time but had to tramp around the north end as there was no trail. We landed at the camp a little after one o'clock. The stove was still warm and the camp record showed that two people had just been there. We rested a few minutes and then hit the good trail south for about a half hour, when we stopped and had a bully meal of rice, bread, ham, cheese, tea, etc.

Zene felt very strong after this so led off and set a pretty good pace. We came on to the Swanson where we stopped and inspected the camp and took some pictures. We made camp from the Swanson in 1 ½ hours and found Sam Mills there. He reported he had been there for two days and the only excitement was that he shot a hedgehog.

Top: The Adirondack League Club camp at the Swanson Stillwater on West Canada Creek. Bottom: (left to right) Zene, Doc, Harve and Ray at the old John Conklin camp just south of the Adirondack League Club line.

Harve and I layed to and got a big meal and then we all visited until about 11:30. Eastman had a terrible pair of blisters on his heels but it did not worry him.

A hard thunderstorm came up in the night and Doc allowed that the wrath of God was liable to be visited on the camp and the unrighteous gang. We all turned in at 11:30.

—Bob

Sunday August 24th.

Sunday, the day of rest. Everyone was quite willing to take things easy after the hike back from Northrup the day before and a good loaf was had by all. I took a much needed bath and did a bit of family washing also shaved and left on mustache, sideburns and beard so as not to have so much to take off. The rest of the gang were more ambitious and took them all off, much shouting from the front porch and marvelous exhibitions of poor marksmanship—Big feeds to wipe out the memory of short rations on Northrup: also quite a novelty and pleasure to again have a plate to eat from and knife, fork and spoon to use. Late in the afternoon I went up to the rifts and caught one trout, just so as not to be skunked for the day. In the evening Zene gave an exhibition of long distance talking. Bob and Doc sneaked off to bed about 9:30. The rest of us stuck it out till 11:30. Zene was still going strong but after some maneuvering Harve managed to sneak up behind and hit him on the head with a club. Two clouts were required and in the momentary lull in the flow of words we beat it for our beds. Safely under the covers we heard a muttering in the other room, "Gentlemen," Zene was saying, "the soft coal industry in this country is in a state of chaos."

R.F.D. [Ray]

The West Canada above the camp.

Monday, August 25th.

Last night we had a hard thunder and lightning storm and when I awoke this morning it was raining hard. I looked around to see who was missing from the beds and saw that Doc and Zene were up getting breakfast. It was a fishy looking morning but was very hot and muggy.

Five grosbeaks came into the kitchen and hopped around the floor near the door, picking up the crumbs out of the cracks. We watched them through the living room door for several minutes. They had a good feed, chirping to each other as they ate. One at a time they flew out the door until there was but one left. He stayed for some time picking away until at last he looked up and let out a couple of loud chirps as though surprised to find himself alone and then followed the others.

Ray tried fishing in front of the camp but this time with no success. I've heard that one has to know the West Creek well in order to get a mess of trout. You have to know the cold beds at the mouths of little streams and you have to know when to fish there according to the temperature of the weather.

As Doc had pictures of himself working for several hours getting his car out of the mud where he had left it when he came in, he was somewhat anxious to get started. Zene assured him there was nothing to worry about as he would just slip on Doc's tump line and pull the car out as easy as nothing. As Sam was going out at the same time, Doc suggested that Sam run his Essex in and pull him out. I know Sam did not warm up to that idea very much as he had left his Essex at Nobleboro and walked up so as not to have to drive over the very road where Doc got stuck.

About ten o'clock Doc, Zene and Sam left camp. Sam certainly looked funny with his sailor's white hat and that little midget pack basket bobbing up and down on the back of his army knapsack.

In the middle of the afternoon Fritz Neu and Bill Cline came in. Bob prepared a good meal for them and then took them up on Honnedaga

Outlet for a little fishing. They got twenty-three of the size which the Outlet is noted for.

I stayed around camp all day just loafing and again after a day or two in camp was itching to shoulder a pack and hit the trail and sleep on the boughs under canvas—sit around the evening camp fire, bundle up to go to bed and get up in the morning before the sun's warmth has had any effect on the dew on the grass and the mists blowing across the water— That's life. Tomorrow we are going to Metcalf—or somewhere.

—Harve

Tuesday, August 26th.

Got up very late this a.m. and took plenty of time for a fine breakfast.

We deliberated for some time as to just what we wanted to do. Just as we were finishing breakfast, two fellows came up the trail and stopped for a little visit. They were going on up to the Conklin Camp to cut wood. One was an old fellow and the other about 40 years old. They told us the Metcalf was very uncertain fishing but there were some very large trout there. They mentioned Twin Rock Lake as being much better than Metcalf.

After they went on we finally decided to go up the Indian to the old Miller Camp and on to Twin Rock. We were in no particular hurry. We took our time to fix up the camp and do a few little odd jobs.

Old Peachy Barse had sent us some wax beans so we cooked them and some carrots and, with what rice pudding we had left, we made a good meal about noon.

We carefully divided our duffel into four packs and at 1:10 left the camp. When we came by the Conklin Camp we found our two friends just eating lunch. They had cut no wood as yet and did not feel very ambitious as they had stopped with Peachy Barse the night before and had indulged in some White Mule.

We visited a few minutes and then came on. We hit the Indian at 2:20 and took the old tote road up on the mountain. It was a warm afternoon and we took it slow. We hit an old beaver dam after we had gotten up on the mountain but there were no beavers and some one had torn out the dam. We crossed over the old dam and pushed on in the woods until we came to a split in the trail. We took the left hand one and in a short time came out into a big burning. Fire had been in it this year. I scared up a big hawk, but then saw that our hawk was a big eagle.

Ray explored all around and finally came back and reported a good place to camp on the north side of the burning and also reported the river there and a wide water.

In the burning I found a beautiful little stream of cold water running through the grass. The little stream looked fishy but there was nothing doing.

We found the remains of an old log dam at the foot of the still water and also a good spot to camp so we pitched the tent. About this time I sneaked out a few hundred feet to where the little cold stream came into the big stream and found a wonderful cold bed. The first cast I made I landed a trout and then for the next few minutes I did some real fishing. I called to the gang and every one put his rods together and took a crack at it. It was about dark when we quit fishing so we finished the camp and got supper by candle light.

It was a peach of a night and the stars were very bright. Mars came up over the mountain and we sat around the fire and decided that Mars was inhabited and that there was trout-fishing there.

—Bob

The spring hole which gave up so many trout. X is the place to stand.

Wednesday, August 27th.

Five men sleeping in Harve's tent made rather a full house and the end-men were rather near the big out-doors. Bob slept at one end of the line and Harve at the other. Now Bob weighs 200 and Harve 130 so it would be easy to guess which one was moved, in the turning and hunching during the night. Anyway, along in the night some time, we were all awakened by an outburst of cussing and grumbling from Harve who had awakened from the cold to find himself pushed almost completely under the edge of the tent out into the cold, cold night. He must have figured that since there was no room on his end of the line there must be some at the other; so he went around on Bob's end and sure enough he found plenty of space there and crawled in and finished the night there.

It was just peep of day when I opened my eyes and stuck my head out of the tent. Everything cold and dripping with dew, and the burning covered with mist. The east was brightening and the brightest stars were just fading out. The moon was riding high and the spruce stood out black across the stream. I soon had a fire started and throwing out a grateful warmth; and there was no sign of life from the four sleepers within the tent.

We already had plenty of trout for breakfast but the stream with the mist rolling along its surface looked too inviting. I took my rod and made my way through the heavy dripping grass to the spring hole where we had fished the night before. The trout were ready and, while the sun came up over the horizon, I landed eight, one after another. Meanwhile, there showed signs of activity about the tent and, when I returned, breakfast was ready, with trout as the main item. This disposed of, we struck our tent and putting all our duffel in the baskets we hid the whole outfit in the woods nearby for we intended coming back there that night. For we certainly didn't want to take any chance of a club warden finding our camp set-up on the preserve. Our permit was to cross, not to camp on the preserve. We crossed the Indian River at the site of the old lumber dam and followed an old tote road along the northern side.

It was full of windfalls and hard going. There were no signs that anyone had been over it in years. In about half an hour we crossed the river again on the rocks and a few minutes' walk from there brought us to the site of the old Miller Camp. This camp was burned about two years ago and there is nothing there now except the clearing in which it stood. We prowled around at the place where the camp had stood, now grown up to berry bushes, picking up now and then a rusty tool or dish and gathering an idea of what the place had been. We lunched here and caught a few grasshoppers in the grassy clearing.

Continuing on up the river over a fair trail, in a few minutes we crossed the club line and were again on state land. In about twenty minutes we came to a stillwater that looked trouty. We jointed our rods and caught eight all small. In the meantime, black clouds rolled up and thunder began to rumble but luckily the worst of it passed us by. It was now about three

The camp in the burning on the Indian River.

o'clock and high time for us to be getting back to the place we had left our outfit. We retraced our steps to the Miller Camp and a short distance beyond and swung into an old tote road, keeping to the south of the river. This we found skirted the burning on which we had camped the night before. This burning incidentally is several hundred acres in extent and easy to travel, being burned clean.

We were soon back to the old camp site and in a few minutes the outfit was brought out of its hiding place and the tent was up. And with little time to spare, for the sky was again filling with black clouds and the thunder was rumbling. This time we were in the storm's direct path. Everything seemed to take on a ghastly greenish color. With the rain came the wind. We looked out through a narrow slit in the front of the tent to see the rain coming down in sheets and the trees bending below the gale. The tent trembled as blast after blast struck it. There were few distinct claps of thunder. It was a continuous rumble and roar. And through it all, the air, the trees, the grass—everything, even the few flames of the fire which had not died out before the rain, showed a pale coppery greenish color. So the storm passed over, all outside the tent soaked and all inside dry and comfortable.

After the rain we prepared our supper. I did a little fishing but have forgotten whether I caught anything or not. All I remember is that storm. The stars were now out and a peaceful night was ahead. Soon five of us were pounding our ears in true and accepted form.

R.F.D. [Ray]

Thursday, August 28th.

Early in the morning Raymond crawled out and started a good fire. We got up half an hour or so later and saw him fishing at the stillwater. I think he caught seven before we had breakfast. The last part of our two breakfasts on the burning was the cup of blueberries with sugar and milk. Every one smacked his lips for more. After breakfast I took the camera and took a walk across the burning with a definite picture in view. I wanted the sky line of evergreen on the edge of the burning.

After I exposed for this I took one of the streams in the grass with the spire top balsams in the background. I was very favorably impressed with the subjects when I exposed for them. They looked like winners but the time to talk is after the films are developed and printed.

Top: (Left to right) Bill Cline, Fritz, Harve and Ray enjoy a trout breakfast topped off with blueberries. Bottom: Bill and Harve begin breaking down the camp.

We packed up our stuff and left at 9:30. A little trouble was had in following the trail just as we left the burning as we had kept a little too far to the left.

On the trail I noticed holes in a balsam about a foot or so from the ground. They evidently were made by a woodpecker but the chips were so large that it aroused my curiosity. The largest of the holes was a good four inches across and some of the chips were fully that size. I believe it must have been made by that large woodpecker, the "Cock o' the woods." This bird is becoming very rare.

We hiked along the trail like Kipling's "Boots, boots, boots, boots," until we hit the Indian a few hundred feet above where it empties into the West Creek. A half mile down the West Creek from here, the trail following a large part of the way on top of a long narrow hogsback, we came to the cable crossing. On the small car suspended on the cable by two iron wheels we rode across the stream. The car had to make five trips as the seat could hold but one man. A long manila rope on pulleys made it possible for the men on either bank to pull the car. When I was in midstream with my pack basket back of me on the seat, those at the ends of the cable began swinging it sideways, each swing sending me higher, the same time they would pull me ahead a little. I hung tight to the iron frame and my feet swung loosely. The rocks below looked like a hard place to land. It was a wild ride.

Harve on the cable crossing.

When we passed the Conklin Camp the two men were out cutting wood and we did not stop. We arrived at Trume's Camp at 12:30 and as Bill and Fritz were going out, we immediately prepared a real meal.

When Bill and Fritz went out Raymond and I went along with them as far as the old lumber camp at the head of Seabury Stillwater. When they came in, Bill lost his pipe somewhere en route and it was a queer streak of luck that he picked it up on the way out.

Supper was ready to serve when we returned. Bob had prepared a pot of sliced potatoes and ham and baked it in the oven. I don't know what he called it or exactly how it was fixed but, as they say in Sweden—it was the raspberries.

We had had a hard crowded bed for a couple of nights and I knew how good the spring bed would feel, but before turning in I picked up a piece of an old Syracuse newspaper that Fritz Neu had brought in and read about LaFollett and the proximity of Mars.

After getting in bed I looked out of the window and Mars was just coming up over the mountain across the creek.

—Harve

Friday, August 29th.

Somehow it was very hard to get up today. Ray was out first, I came second and Harve came to at 8:30. We had a very heavy breakfast and then decided to do a lot of odd jobs about the Camp. I put a new board in the porch floor to replace one chewed in two by the hedge hogs. Ray started to pile up the wood that was lying all over the place. He worked several hours and then I gave him a hand. We finished the job in the afternoon. I also split up a lot of wood. Harve took a long walk down the creek and over the west mountain, he said to get some pictures. He returned about 6 p.m. and said that he was lost. How he could be lost when he had his compass with him was more than Ray and I could figure out. We checked him up on the films and found that he had taken one picture.

About 1 p.m. the two fellows who had been up in the Conklin Camp cutting wood came back. They stopped for about an hour and had a bite to eat with Ray and me. They gave us a loaf of white bread which was very acceptable.

The younger man had been working at Beaver River and told us all about it. They are going to burn the old Club House.

Late last night Ray and Harve put on some sketch trying to shoot a hedge hog. Each night after we would retire we would be visited by hedge hogs who would chew the boards in the porch. We had retired and were just about asleep when the gnawing started. Ray and Harve very quietly got up and one got the flashlight and the other the gun. When they made a little noise the hedge hog would stop and then they would wait for a few minutes for the hedge hog to start again.

They finally got to the door and then Ray gave the signal. The door flew open and they marched out on the porch in record time. Ray said "Flash the light quick." Harve said "Where is it? I haven't got it." So there they stood in the dark with a gun and heard Mr. Hedge Hog run off through the woods. Then each bawled the other out and finally they came back to bed and as I began to kid them they began to laugh. Then they got organized right and later when the Hedge Hog came back they got one shot at him but missed it.

—Bob

I made a little remark when we were starting for Northrup about "Doc had a tump line and Zene had a pack," which Doc picked up and said it would be the start of some poetry. Harve and I doped out something which goes like the following:

Doc had a tump line and Zene had a pack
    Bob had a heavy load all on his back
Harve plugged along chocked full of good cheer.
    While Ray very thoughtful brought up the rear.

The morning was lovely and the atmosphere fine
    And the start it was made at just quarter to nine.
The trail was a fair one except a few spots
    Where it was full of big windfalls, mudholes and rocks.

The six miles to Swanson was made in fine shape
    But there we slowed up on account of our freight.
Doc's heels gave some bother on account of his boots
    Which had rubbed off the skid and they looked like the deuce.

We pushed up the mountain and then crossed a stream
    The sky clouded over and it started to rain.
We stopped a few minutes to take a small bite
    And Ray said, "By Gosh, fellows, we'll get a wet night".

The Otter Lake camp which was reached in due time
    Afforded us shelter from an hour and a half's rain.
We then tramped around the head of the lake
    And tried hard to figure the best trail to take.

It was some awful going I'll have to admit
    But with good fishing in prospect we never would quit.
The thunder and the lightning and the rain all let loose
    And, By Gosh, I thought we would never reach Goose.

But after a soaking and mud up to our knees
    We finally saw Goose Lake loom through the trees
Ray picked out a spot on which to make camp
    And the flow of Zene's language darned near dried off the map.

So we had a fine supper and a big bed of boughs
    And with a fire burning brightly we were soon in a doze
And we dreamed of fair weather and of Northrup Lake
    And the wonderful trout we expected to take.

Now Northrup is famous, as Trume Haskell knows,
    And it's full of big trout as far as it goes,
Pink bellied trout have made its reputation
    But pink or white bellied it's the same recreation
So we landed a few without hesitation
    We landed about ten- wait I am all out of rhyme
I'll bung up this verse if I don't take my time.

T'was a trip well worth while with plenty of trout
    And we felt well repaid as we took the trail out
With compass and map we traced our way back
    Doc with his tump line and Zene with his pack.

—*Bob & Harve*

Saturday, August 30th.

This a.m. Ray allowed as to how there ought to be some good fishing up the Outlet Brook as Mason Burleigh had had wonderful luck up there in the spring and also he had heard some great tales as to what was in Baby Lake, the outlet of which is Outlet Brook.

So we took the last of the worms and got together a nice lunch and started about ten o'clock. We traveled up the stream intending to start in somewhere near the little falls but Bob wouldn't wait so he started in where Jones Lake Outlet comes in. He found a good pool up there and connected with several fair trout. He finally came back to the main stream and followed up until he caught up with Ray and Harve.

On the way up the stream Ray was leading, Bob second and Harve third, in single file. Just after Ray passed through a little clump of bushes, Bob noticed a few hornets and, on looking further, he discovered a large hornet nest about two feet from the ground. He gave it

The pools under the big rocks always give up one and Ray is just about to connect.

a kick with his foot and ran on up the trail. One hornet got Bob on the right shoulder before he got away and Harve ran back down the trail and then took a big detour, all the time saying something about a fool stunt and what ought to happen to Bob.

About two o'clock we reached the little falls and then had lunch. Harve took several pictures and finally we agreed to push on upstream toward Baby Lake. The going was a little bad but every little while we would pull a nice trout out of some hole.

We reached the remains of an old dam at the foot of a still water and on climbing over the spill way saw a very nice camp or log house and a little shack. We made an inspection of the whole place and found it belonged to some Rochester fellows.

The Rochester camp on the old Stillwater.

There wasn't very much water in the stream and the fishing at this place was nothing much to speak about.

We took a picture and then went on upstream through some very nice woods until we came to a large pool. Ray fished this and got 2 or 3 good ones. Bob went on up the stream and finally came to the foot of a very high falls. He then looked things over a little and then came back to where Ray and Harve were. He reported the falls as 75 ft. high but Ray said he ought to put a decimal point between the 7 and the 5 and Harve was inclined to agree to this also. However, the falls were very pretty and the water here is very clean, it being one of the few clear water streams in the Adirondacks, most of the water being dark from tamarack and hemlock and other soft wood. We finally reached the log camp and stopped a few minutes when we took down our rods.

A little side stream.

We figured out that there must be a better trail or at least better walking in the east side of the stream so we made a start. After we crossed over we found a fairly good trail and followed it on down the creek to the old hunter's camp and from there to our own camp. It took us just 1½ hours to reach camp when we arrived at 7 p.m.

Ray proceeded to clean the fish and we found we had 28—some very fair ones, so we had some for supper.

Supper was a good meal that night and we laid to it for fair.

—*Bob*

Sunday, August 31st.

Sometime last night another hedgehog sketch was pulled off. The first thing I knew about it was three or four shots just outside the window. "Did you get him?" I hollered.

Raymond had heard a hedgehog and got up and, with the gun and flashlight, had sneaked quietly out on the porch. With the lighted flash lying on the porch floor he opened up on Mr. Hedgehog who went off the end of the porch and under the camp. This morning we pulled him out deader than a door nail. The place looked like a hunting camp with the two dead hedgehogs on the front porch.

This evening as I was writing the log I asked:

"What happened this morning?"

"Nuthin", was the answer.

"What happened today anyway?"

"Nuthin', nuthin' doin.'"

That's the kind of a day it was, a quiet Sunday. Ray went over all his fishing tackle and had his lines out to dry, stretching them for a hundred feet or more in front of the camp.

For some unknown reason, except that there was a flat iron in camp, Bob pressed his pants. He intends to catch the train for Albany that leaves Utica just ahead of the Empire[10] but I don't think anyone on that train will ever know that Bob pressed his pants.

It was a boiling hot day. I put the rocking chair in the doorway in the little breeze that there was and sat there and looked out on the stream. A large shadow swept across the porch and I looked up and saw a great blue heron about seventy-five feet in the air flying south right over the center of the stream. It was like an aero plane following a water course route.

A kingfisher sitting on the cable crossing let out with that jackass-like laugh of his and I watched a wren as he bobbed around the woodpile.

About four o'clock the swallows came out. There seemed to be hundreds of them and they were flying very high. They must be tree swallows.

Aside from these and an occasional cry of a blue jay the wild life which I observed from my rocking chair were many dragon flies, bees, black flies, mosquitoes and numerous queer looking bugs, some of which were marked in black and red and orange, as wonderful as any part of King Tut's tomb. Along towards evening the mosquitoes got so bad that we had to start two smudge pots going.

---

[10] The Empire State Express, a fast, first-class New York Central train.

I also noticed three different kinds of flowers growing near the front porch and pondered on my ignorance as I did not know the names of any of them.

Tomorrow we go out. With long faces we packed up our personal belongings. Ray and Bob each wanted to wet a line once more in the main stream but finally called it quits for the year. We laid aside a few things for Peachy Barse to give to him on our way out, some coffee, macaroni, rice and cocoa. Tonight for supper we had our last feed of trout and they were of great flavor and good size, being the largest of those we caught yesterday on Honnedaga Outlet. When Bob was eating one of the trout, he glanced up at a map on the wall of the Adirondacks, showing a blue line boundary of the Adirondack Park and said, "How would you like to take out the ten largest trout within that blue line?"—Well, that's the way it goes.

Twas a quiet Sunday and "nuthin' doin."

—*Harve*

Trume Haskell's camp as seen from West Canada Creek.
Tomorrow we go out.

Monday, September 1st—Labor Day.

We were up at about daylight and had a fine breakfast. Then we got busy. Harve and Ray put all the bedding away, swept up the bedroom and the upstairs and then fastened up the windows. I washed the dishes and put them away and cleared up the kitchen and got everything in its place. We had plenty of time to do a good job and we did it.

When we got our packs all ready they seemed to be very heavy but we finally snapped the lock in the door, took a final drink from the spring and started away from camp at 10 minutes of nine.

We took it easy on the way out only resting a few minutes until we reached the old lumber camp at the head of the stillwater. Here we stopped and made a thorough inspection and figured out just how we were going to fix it up after we bought it.

Where Harve is liable to locate any time.

Bob, twenty years hence.

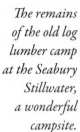

The remains of the old log lumber camp at the Seabury Stillwater, a wonderful campsite.

We finally went on a few hundred feet to the camp of a fellow by the name of Simmons. He is an official of the G. E. Co. at Schenectady.

Old Barse was then cutting brush so we all had a little visit. We left Peachy some coffee and a few other articles of food and then came on to the foot of the still water where old Peachy's camp is located. We inspected this and the old dam, took some pictures and then pushed along down the trail which is very pretty along the creek. We made only one stop before we reached the flat rock in the road. We had agreed to meet Clemmons at just noon so we had to hurry a little.

We reached Trume's old place at just 2 minutes past noon and found Clemmons's man with a Ford car. He said he had been there 20 minutes. We looked over the Ford, filled her up with water and piled in.

Old Peachy had told us that Dan Clemmons said he was going to have a nice chicken dinner for us as we had paid him well and he wanted us to come again. We were a little disappointed at not seeing Dan so we asked his man where he was. He said Dan had to go to Herkimer but he expected him back so we still figured on a chicken dinner.

We got our packs in the Ford and then piled in and started down the road, getting to Clemmons's place about one o'clock. We didn't see anything of Dan or the chicken dinner and no one seemed to be home. We got Harve's car out of the barn and unhooded the Ford. About this time Mrs. Clemmons came home and we asked her how much we owed Mr. Clemmons for bringing us down in the Ford. She said, "Oh, I don't

*Mrs. Dan
Clemmons.*

know, he said you could give whatever you thought it was worth." We
finally asked her how Five Dollars would do and she said it would be
all right so we gave her the five. She looked it all over and we could not
tell whether she was surprised that we had given so much or too little.
We finally agreed that Old Dan usually handled all the money and that
all his wife had to do was to work and run the house.

She said as it was Labor Day most of the folks had gone to a little
party and her husband had to go to Herkimer. She then offered to get
us something to eat but we decided we would go on to Barneveld or
Utica.

I took a couple of pictures of the place and promised to send her a
copy, all of which seemed to please her very much.

We then drove on to Barneveld keeping to the north of the reservoir.
We found Trume and paid him for the camp and then drove on to Utica,
getting there at 3:00 p.m. I left at 3:20 after saying goodbye to Ray and
Harve.

We figured out the expense of the trip and it had cost us less than
$20.00 each. We had caught about 175 trout. Altogether we had all the
fish we could eat and we had not thrown any away.

We agreed that the trip was well worth while and one of the best we
had ever taken. We further agreed that we would try to get a permanent place all our own to build just the kind of a camp we want.

—Bob

Chapter 15
Segoolie!
A Camp of Our Own

The old camp beside the Seabury Stillwater during the winter of 1928–1929.

T O MAKE GOOD ON THEIR PLEDGE ". . . to get a permanent place all our own to build just the kind of a camp we want. . . ." they let Trume Haskell know of their interest in buying one of the old run-down camps they saw on the way home from West Canada Creek, either that, they told him, or they would consider a piece of property to build on, if one came up for sale.

Trume was the right person to tell. His roots ran deep in the West Canada Valley. His dad, "Pony" Haskell, had driven a buckboard for "Big Eve" of Nobleboro and used the earnings to set up a hotel and a bar at the old Wilkinson place on West Canada Creek in the 1880s. In that environment, Trume met all the notable characters of the period. He was even known to pal around with the hermit French Louie.

Trume's influence paid off the following spring when a little log cabin on a one-acre parcel became available. Coincidentally, it was one of the same cabins that Bob and Harve had inspected on the way home from Trume's on Labor Day 1924, the "old lumber camp at the head of the stillwater."

There may have been no time for Bob to enlist the help of his friends in the purchase, or maybe they didn't have the money to pitch in, but Bob didn't hesitate. He jumped at the opportunity and bought the camp from local land mogul Henry C. Ballou, the son of Theodore Ballou, a co-founder of the big gang mills at Hinckley back in 1848. It wasn't much land to the Ballous, who at one point owned upwards of 28,000 acres in the region, but it was exactly what the men had envisioned, a camp on a hill overlooking West Canada Creek at the head of the Seabury Stillwater and a "stone's throw" from Trume Haskell's place. From this camp all of the fun and fishing they had experienced the summer before would be accessible to them whenever they could get there.

There isn't much information about the goings-on over the next few years, but they must have made some work trips and soon had the camp in a nice, livable condition. And it was probably planned all along—or maybe that's how long it took Harve and Ray to save enough money— but in July 1928, Bob sold a third of the property each to Harve and Ray, making them all equal partners in the camp.

It was around that time that they also decided to name the camp. The unusual word "Segoolie" was selected (how we don't know) and the word soon became their favorite greeting as well as their camp name. From then on, instead of saying "hello" when they met, or beginning a letter "Dear Harve," they simply said, or wrote, "Segoolie!" But what exactly did it mean and where did it come from? A newspaper article that hung on the wall of the old Camp Segoolie helped to explain. It appeared in the *Utica Observer-Dispatch* on March 7, 1949:

Segoolie

This is a story of a camp, Indians and a boxing match.

It is custom among many persons in Central New York who have camps to give them names. Harvey Dunham, Irving Place, Utica, has such a camp on the West Canada Creek and he calls it Segoolie, an Indian expression.

Dunham's brother, Ray, of Syracuse brought a number of neighbors to spend a number of days at Segoolie, which they enjoyed very much.

Sometime after, one of the neighbors went to a boxing match in which one of the fighters was an Indian from the nearby reservation. Along with him in the bleachers was a good sized group of fellow tribesmen.[11]

Suddenly the Indian boxer tore into his opponent, and the men from the reservation rose to a man and began yelling: "Segoolie! Segoolie! Segoolie!"

And did that surprise the Syracusan, the Indians yelling out the name of Dunham's camp up on "West Creek."

That was later explained. The word means, "Keep at it," "Keep going," or "Keep up the good work."

So you see, the original Americans knew as well as anybody what it takes to get anywhere.

Wherever it came from, the unusual name stuck and Camp Segoolie became that "place all their own," a piece of the good life for Bob, Ray, Harve, their families and friends up on West Canada Creek.

[11] We replaced a potentially offensive reference to Native Americans with the phrase "fellow tribesmen."

Chapter 16
Fraser Clearing

The old camp at Fraser Clearing and the sign that hung over the door.

IN THE SPRING OF 1929, another interesting property on West Canada Creek became available and a business idea was hatched. Henry Ballou, the previous owner of Segoolie, had passed away in 1927, and many of his real estate holdings were beginning to hit the market. Among them was a two-and-a-half-acre lot known as "Fraser Clearing," situated at the opposite end of the same Stillwater that Segoolie overlooked. It was only a one-mile paddle away and it, like the Segoolie property, had a usable log cabin still standing. Alongside the cabin were the remains of an old lumber camp in decay, but from the ruins the men estimated that a good amount of building material could be salvaged—maybe even enough to build another camp.

"The Clearing" had some history going for it too. Besides being the site of some of the earliest lumber camps in the region, it had also once been home to Johnny Leaf, the notorious St. Regis Mohawk who was well known for his willingness to kill a deer for a pint of whiskey. Johnny's prowess as a hunter, his love of liquor, and his fiery temper kept his stories alive in West Canada Valley folklore. Fraser Clearing was one of the last places Johnny lived before he was killed in a lumberjacks' brawl after several days of heavy drinking. Johnny's connection to the property only added to its allure.

After thoughtful deliberation, Bob and Harve decided to buy the lot to start a rental business with the two camps. After all, how hard would it be to entice the "city sports" back home to come up to the wild West Canada country, given all the tall tales and wonderful adventures that they could share about the area? Who could resist such sport? It would surely be a winner.

The decision was made. On June 24, 1929, the sale closed. Fraser Clearing was theirs. They now had a second camp to fix up and a ramshackle mess of broken-down buildings to salvage material from.

The ruins of the barn next door to Segoolie probably looked a lot like the ruins salvaged at Fraser Clearing.

In the fall of 1929, Harve made a Christmas card for the Gillespies that celebrated
their "West Creek" purchases. The original artwork was 18 inches tall and included
Harve's illustration and several photographs pasted to a board. The picture in the
center is of Segoolie and the pictures at the bottom are of the Seabury Stillwater
in winter and summer. A hearty camp breakfast of trout, coffee and pancakes is
pictured in the center. The original piece hung on the wall at Segoolie until the
cabin was burned down in 1985. The timbers had rotted beyond repair.

The view near the head of the Seabury Stillwater.

By the time hunting season started in 1929, Bob and Harve may have begun questioning the timing of their purchase of Fraser Clearing. The dust was settling after the big stock market crash in October and a sense of uncertainty gripped the nation. What calamity was next? The whole idea of making the camps into a successful business venture might not be so easy after all. Bob's situation was pretty secure. The telephone industry was booming and his job was in no danger, but prospects were not as good for Harve and Ray. The Great Depression had begun.

Through that winter and into spring, working on the camps was a nice diversion from the economic collapse that was in full swing nationwide. There was always a job to do at camp—not so for the thousands of workers getting laid off from their jobs every week. At camp there was wood to cut, salvage to sort through, roofs to patch and chinking to put in between logs. And as soon as the cabin at Fraser Clearing was cleaned up and ready for guests they began building a second camp nearby out of the salvaged materials. They named that camp "Johnny Leaf."

Soon visitors began coming. Friends and family alike were entranced with the rustic charm, splendid scenery and plentiful fish. West Canada Creek was a great place to be in the spring.

SOMETIME THAT SAME SPRING, Harve inherited a piece of property in Amboy, N.Y., near Camden, and decided to try his hand at farming. He planted potatoes and convinced Bob, Ray and two other men to help him plant 2,500 sapling trees in April. Their "pay" for helping out was a trip to nearby Carterville Pond, just north of Panther Lake, to fish. They caught two small trout, a reward that provided a better return on investment than Harve's farm ever would.

By mid-summer Harve realized that it was too expensive and inefficient to be a commuter-farmer, so he hired someone who lived nearby to manage the crops. He drove away and hoped for the best.

The summer of 1930 turned tragically worse on August 11, by an act of random violence. Ray Dunham's wife, Alvine, and his two daughters, Eleanor, 11, and Claire, 3, hopped off a trolley car in the City of Syracuse that day, just as a truck thief began shooting at a motorcycle policeman who was trying to pull him over. In a stroke of horrible luck, a stray bullet hit Alvine in the face, shattering her jaw. Though extremely serious, Alvine's injuries were not life-threatening. She survived, but Ray's work to help his family through a difficult physical and psychological recovery was just beginning.

Things were a little brighter for the Gillespie family. Bob's daughter was about to be married. Carolyn Malkin, Bob's granddaughter, shared the story as it was told to her years later. It was the story of her parents' honeymoon in August 1930.

The wedding was on Salina Street and Mother and Daddy left for the honeymoon. Now my great-grandmother, my grandparents and my aunt all were going to go on the honeymoon, only the women said that was not a good idea. But my grandfather said, "No, we're going to go." So their first night was spent in a hotel in Utica, and they arrived unexpectedly to surprise Mother and Daddy. They all stayed at the same hotel in Utica. The next day they all drove out to Segoolie on the honeymoon. I don't know much else about the scheme other than that Mother and Daddy were most surprised. Grandpa and Grandmother stayed at Segoolie while Mother and Daddy went over to one of the cabins at Fraser Clearing. That was the start of their honeymoon.

Chapter 17
Playing in Hard Luck

Harve and Bob enjoy lunch at Belden Vly, a long but worthwhile walk.

AFTER TWO UNPROFITABLE YEARS, Harve resolved that farming was not his calling. West Canada Creek was where his heart was and that was where he'd have his best shot at making a little extra money. To accomplish that he and Bob decided to build another camp and to get busy marketing the property better.

The new camp would be called Eagle's Nest because of its commanding view of the valley from the hill above the Clearing and it would need to be built from mostly new lumber because the salvaged timbers from the old buildings had all been used. As part of their planning, Harve created a breakdown of costs in this letter he sent to Bob. It gives a sense of how much it cost to build a small cabin back then, as well as a sense of how much things have changed. The letter was undated.

Dear Bob.

This looks good. Figuring the best, 2 x 6 rafters too. We'll buy the roofing from Clarence. The carpenter wants $100 to put it up. He's a good man and will do a good job but no man will do a good job in fly time. I told him he could live at Segoolie or on the job. Suit himself. He knows it's a mile from Segoolie. Will also get a price from Blue on trucking to Wrights. If Thomas will truck for the same price will give the trucking job to Thomas. Is Wright okay or shall we dicker at Nobleboro for Dan Clemmons. It is two loads for a small truck or one load for a 5 ton truck.

I planted Blue Spruce at Segoolie. They are too good for the farm. I have 3,000 to plant at the farm about May 1st.

It's going to be a big spring alright. We must support our roof at Segoolie more. It might not break, but the rafters will bend slowly and in several years will show a decided sag in the roof. We can put supports in some way but not to interfere with our space too much.

The whole family is going over to Jim Kiblers tonight to a movie show. Jim brought a machine home and several reels.

Was down to the Isaac Walton Club meeting last night. Nothing of importance because they had their sportsmen's exhibit.

I am going to take my four blankets to an awning man tomorrow to have them sewed together and get a light duck cover. It's going to be a regular sleeping bag.

Tell Raymond that one of my snowshoes is bowed like an old fashioned chopping bowl and I was wondering how it would be to soak them good in water and let them dry out slowly. I think they dried too fast.

I'll see you at Little Rock along about noon.

Harve

Eagle's Nest cabin, overlooking Fraser Clearing.

Harve's estimate for building Eagle's Nest:

Sills: 100 feet of 2 x 6

Plates: 40 feet of 2 x 6 and 70 of feet 2 x 4

Ridge Poles: 24 feet of 1 x 6

Rafters: 16 pieces 2 x 6 x 16

Studs and Joists: 580 feet of 2 x 4 and 5 pieces 2 x 6 x 16

Roof Boards: 400 feet of pine boards

Flooring: 245 feet spruce boards

Siding: 465 feet (6 inch wide)

1 Door Frame

1 Cas Mul Frame

1 Cas Frame for pair sliding sash 9 light, 6 x 10

5 Barn Sash 9 light 8 x 10

1 Exterior door pine

Facing: 32 feet of 1 x 5 spruce

Roof Edging: 100 feet 1 x 2 spruce

Total about 2200 feet besides windows and frames

Total Cost $144.44 plus $100 labor.

Later that summer, Bob wrote to Harve about some financial matters. The letter shows how much pennies mattered at the time.

July 19, 1932
Segoolie:

I am writing Wilbur Ralph about the stove. I will also write
Dan Clemmons and tell him to get it for us and take it down to the
Clearing. As to the booking. Here is what I did. You fix it up and
tell me what to do.

I sent you $2.50. You spent .88 for lumber for Segoolie. I gave you
$15 from that rental. We each put in a dollar toward the stove for the
Clearing. You said something about the next $5 I will receive from
the camps. Now look—as long as you are playing in hard luck, why
don't I send you all the receipts from the Clearing. I'd just as soon
do this. I have two or three good prospects for week end parties as
soon as the flies let up.

Here is something else. . . . Why don't you make up a little sketch
of some kind that will be a sort of advertisement and I will get it
photographed and make up a bunch of post cards and mail them to
all of my woods bugs friends.

I got your key to the log camp. I'll mail it tomorrow.
So long,
Bob

Though it may have been a test of Harve's pride to accept Bob's
charity, it may also have been comforting to have the support of a
faithful friend.

Harve got to work right away designing ads as Bob suggested, and
the series of quirky maps he created squarely captured the fun, fresh
air and sporting adventure that awaited visitors to Fraser Clearing or
Segoolie. He made the north woods along the mighty West Canada
look like a great place to be.

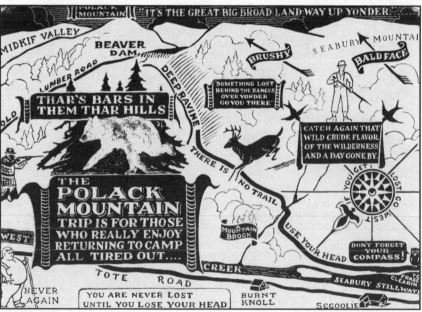

With equipment available at his office, Bob took care of making copies of the flyers. He even mentioned his clandestine activities in a letter to his daughter, "I went down to the office and ran a bunch of prints through

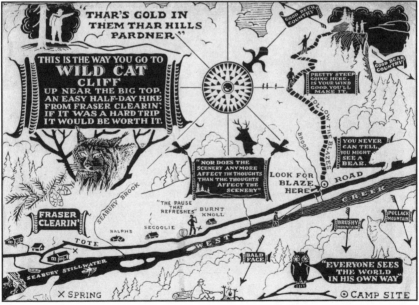

the blue print machine. Harve and I are peddling them out to prospective patrons of the Clearing. Hope we can do some business this year. You see I get these prints for 100% discount so it's cheap advertising."

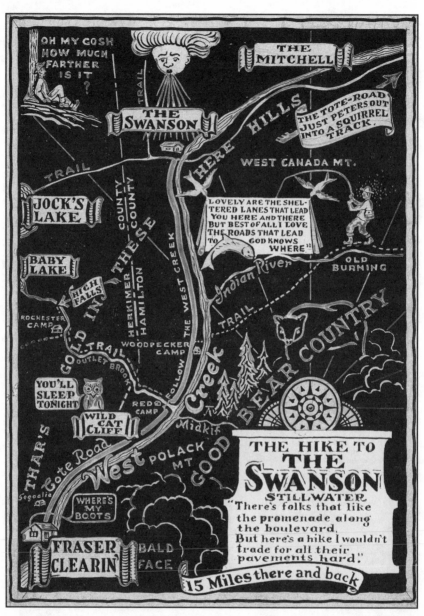

Bob's job in Syracuse had become as much a lifeline to Harve as it was to him and his family, but it made his trips to West Canada Creek less frequent than he would have liked. Harve, on the other hand, was practically living at Segoolie. It wasn't a problem between good friends

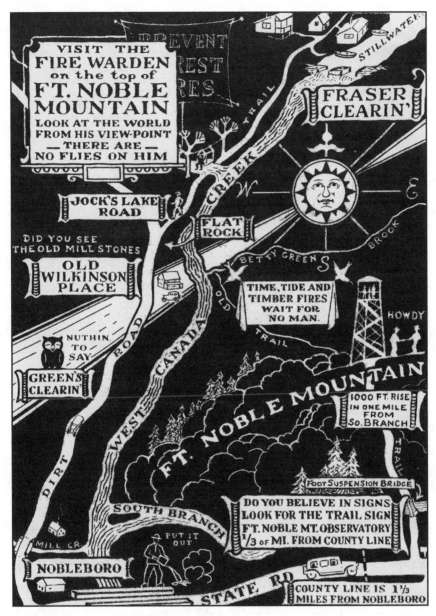

though; it was just that Bob missed it so. He expressed that sentiment in
a note to Harve. "Your two accounts about last weekend were received
yesterday and there is only one thing that should have been there aside
from you . . . and that was me. Lordy Goddy it made me homesick."

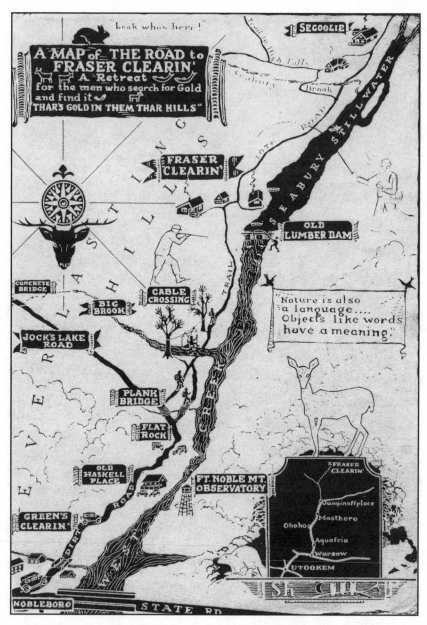

Harve's maps quickly had the desired effect. Bob boasted in a note to Harve that "I just rented one of the cabins for a week next spring to our assistant manager for Auburn. He saw a set of our maps and they sure made a hit with him."

Left and preceeding five pages: The quirky illustrations Harve created to market their camp rentals.

Another potential customer, Charles Phillips, wrote to Bob, "My Dear Mr. Gillespie, I do not know that I should thank you for sending me the maps of Fraser Clearing, since I have not been able to work for the past half hour looking at them."

Through all of 1933, Bob's service to the partnership as a salesman and financier continued, but that suddenly took a turn for the worse. On February 3, 1934, Bob wrote to his daughter Ruth and her husband after a visit with his doctor.

Dear Ruth and Jimmy:

This letter is about a day ahead of time but I have just been down to see [Dr.] Joe Dunnigan and I thought that perhaps you might like to hear what he had to say.

I got the usual going-over and then he told me that the heart muscle had filled in in very good shape and that I probably would find that I would be much better and feel better and that alarm in my chest would let me know that I am getting better and can go a little farther all the time. He told me that next spring I could go into camp and enjoy some fishing but no long tramps and the two things that I must look out for all the time were stairs and hills. I need not be afraid of them, but just to take them very easy and slow. I asked him about using tools and he said that it was O.K. but he didn't mean a sledge hammer or ax or cross-cut saw. He eased up on my medicine and tells me to just watch out. He did ask me if I raised the family or if they raised me and I said, "Both." He did impress on me how lucky I was that I had come through so well and in good shape.

So that's that. Now when spring comes I will have to go to Segoolie and put a rock foundation under the camp and build a root cellar and a new ice house. Eh! What?

Well, Harve went up last week end and left his car at the Green Clearing and it's still there. He couldn't start it and had to walk out to Nobleboro and call Utica and get Jim Kibler to come up and fetch him out. He got the new chunk stove all connected up in Johnny Leaf [and] it heats up the cabin fine. We have a party going in over Feb. 10–12th and we wanted to make sure they would be warm.

Got to read now how Roosevelt's gold policy will not work. I note that they are disappointed in Washington already. Well I hope we can get enough of the cheap dollars to keep going.

So here's luck and good bye so long.

Always,

Dad

Coronary thrombosis was the technical term for the blocked arteries that caused Bob to have a heart attack. Whatever the name for it, his heart was ailing and he knew he'd have to take it easy. His joking about a new foundation, root cellar and ice house at Segoolie only masked his actual desire to get up there and work. His positive demeanor with his daughter was admirable, but he wrote another letter that day to Harve and never even mentioned his health. It hadn't affected his sense of humor at all.

Segoolie:

Last night I gave the girl in the blueprint room a pound of candy and bribed her to mix me up some fresh developer and leave the machine and other stuff where I could get it, and then this a.m. I went down to the office and ran off a lot of prints.

All this kind of advertising costs is time, and I sure have plenty of that. Here we have two holidays this month and not a damn thing to do but stay home.

I think we should put up some more pictures in the little cabins and also a set of the prints. Ray says he will try and dig us up some calendars.

It won't be long now before the sun is shining on both sides of the fence and I just know that business is going to be better and we are going to have a good year at the Clearin'.

So long,

Bob

A year later, Bob's condition worsened. On April 1, 1935, he suffered another heart attack and was ordered to a long bed rest again. By May he was writing again.

May 3, 1935

Segoolie:

Ray said that he just put in a good day cleaning Segoolie. Well, I don't think it hurt either him or Segoolie. My only regret is that I wasn't there to help. They won't let me see anybody yet and I still can't sit up but I am in hopes that the ban will be lifted soon. The doctor tells me that after I get out of this mess I must take a good long rest but I don't see how I can cut much wood on that advice. Ruth is home for a week or two and writing this for me.

Hope to see you soon.

So long,

Bob

While Ruth was home, the family began negotiations on Bob's behalf to purchase a piece of property on the Beaver River in Number Four, N.Y. It wasn't far from old Camp Happy and Salmon Lake, where Bob had traveled so often in better times. The plan was that Bob's younger daughter, Helen, who was the first licensed female architect in Central New York, was to design a log cabin where her father could convalesce nearer to the woods. Carolyn Malkin remembered the story this way:

Grandfather had suffered from heart trouble. He had a heart attack. The doctor said he could not continue to sit at a desk job all week and then hike in to Segoolie and around the woods toting heavy pack baskets on the weekends. My mother and her sister took heed, even if Grandpa didn't. My grandmother, aunt, and mother inquired around and found that Clarence Fisher (Fisher Forestry and Realty Co.) was selling lots on Beaver Lake, and that one could drive right in to the property. It seemed ideal for Grandpa, and Mother and Aunt Helen came up and looked at the lots and chose the ones next door, lots 158 and 159. Grandpa and Grandma actually purchased the property and had the camp built. Aunt Helen designed the log cabin and drew up the plan, but Grandpa and Grandma paid for it all. Jimmy Wilder[12] and "Tiger" Lee did the actual construction.... Both Aunt Helen and Mother—and Grandma too, of course—were anxious to find some place Grandpa could drive to so he could still be in his beloved woods."

After the sale closed, construction got under way quickly that summer of 1935. "Norridgewock" was the name they selected for the cabin meaning "people of the still water between the rapids," an Abenaki Indian term and the name of an Abenaki tribe. It was also the name of the old hotel at Beaver River Station. For whatever reason it was chosen, the location fit the definition. Beaver Lake is actually a large Stillwater of the Beaver River, and a quiet section of water between two faster sections.

Norridgewock, Bob Gillespie's log cabin on the Beaver River.

Bob hoped to be able to spend time at the cabin in September, a desire he mentioned in another letter to Harve:

[12] Jimmy Wilder was Elmer Wilder's cousin.

Syracuse, NY, August 28, 1935

Segoolie:

Your letter came last week and I was more than glad to hear from you and get your reports on the various matters.

First, I'll give you a bit of a report about myself and it isn't a too bad report either, all things considered. I've been sitting up six to seven hours a day for the past two weeks. At first I was so damn weak I couldn't hardly walk at all and when I tried to write I simply could not write a word that anyone could read—I suppose you'll say "Hell, he never could write anyway."

Well last Thursday, the M.D. was here and gave me a good going over and said, "Now let me see you walk." I gave a good exhibition and walked around the dining room table. Then he said "Now Bob, one more exhibition like that and I'll put you back to bed. You ought to know better." Then he asked me when I wanted to take an auto ride, and I said "That's up to you, Doc." He then said if I would regard myself as two hundred years old and act accordingly, I could take a ride Sunday of 15 or 20 miles, and increase it each day on. Then, if there were no ill effects, I could go to the new camp on Labor Day. Well, did that sound good to me!

But isn't that the irony of fate to get this kick in the tail on the opening day of trout fishing and go to the woods on September 2nd? But I am lucky I guess that I am not working on the cinder patch or shoveling coal.[13]

I'll be up there all of September and it all depends on how I get along or how much longer, so I want you to figure on coming up some weekend and seeing your bunk, and I'll give you my share of beans for I can't eat any. So I'll be looking for you.

As to the West Canada—Ray drops in to see me occasionally and he has reported on Segoolie. I wish to God I could be up to Segoolie with about 10 bags of cement and three times that much gravel and a couple of fellows like Ken Clemmons. I would just sit there and put a

---

[13] We think this reference demonstrates that Bob had a heart attack on April 1, 1935, and the cinder patch or shoveling coal meant that he's lucky he didn't die from it and end up in Hades.

foundation under the whole works. But it's the same old story—all we lack is time and money. But the way my doctor and wife are talking, I guess I'll have plenty of time one of these days, for I think they want me to retire. I would retire and live on my pension if I lived in the woods, but I can't do it and live in the city. Of course, that's what I had in mind when I built Norridgewock Camp, so between that and the West Canada, I'll be in good shape, but what the heck will I do with the wife and Helen?

I hope you won't quit writing for the *Outdoorsman* [Magazine.] Your articles are the only good thing in it. Personally, I liked your article in the June issue very much. . . .

I'll bet you have cursed me and my writing all the time you have been reading this, but if you can't make it out, fetch it in with you when you come up to Norridgewock and maybe I can read it for you.

Goodbye,

So long, and luck to you.

Bob

By September, the cabin was ready and Bob was thrilled to be there. On the thirteenth he wrote again to Harve.

"Beaver Lake" No 4. Sept 13, 1935
Segoolie:

Well Pard, I am in the woods at last. A week ago Monday I came up here. Made two stops on the way and took it easy and the very fact that I was coming to the woods helped a lot.

About all I can do is sit on the porch and look around, but that is a damn sight better than being in bed and looking at four walls. I can't do but very little walking, but I sure am feeling much better.

My M.D. told me to stay here until snow flies, so you have got to come up and see the outfit. Come right in the kitchen door without knocking and holler "Segoolie" and you'll be as welcome as the grace of God. I'll be expecting you.

So here is luck—Segoolie,

Bob

At the end of the season, Bob wrote to Harve from Norridgewock one last time.

Beaver Lake No 4. Lewis Co., NY November 4, 1935
Segoolie:

I expect we will be going out of here next Sunday so if you are figuring on coming up you better make it then. But if the weather holds good and there is not too much snow we will come up weekends. Hope to make it four days over Thanksgiving. Do you remember the Thanksgiving you and I spent at Segoolie putting down the floor and we thought we were dead because we couldn't see our breath in Peachy's old camp when we woke up? Gosh a mighty, those days are over for me, but they were great.

It's almost time to think about the Christmas cards. Here's that piece that we found when you were up.

"A campfire in the forest is the most enchanting place on life's highway by which to have a lodging for the night."

Well here's to you. I'll be seeing you soon I hope.

Always,

Bob

Bob passed away eleven days later—another heart attack. He was fifty-eight. His obituary in the telephone company newspaper, *The Upstater*, read in part:

Mr. Gillespie was one of the best-known and best-loved men in the area. Friendliness was an essential part of his nature, and his roster of friends, in the company and out, included all ranks and ages. As division right-of-way supervisor, his position brought him in contact with lawyers and legal processes, and workers and supervisors felt free to call on him for advice and assistance, which he always gave gladly.

Few men loved the woods and mountains better than Mr. Gillespie. He was never happier than when hunting and fishing, or roaming the woods for any reason. Week-ends, whenever possible, and vacations for many years were spent at "Segoolie," a log camp in the Adirondacks, north of Nobleboro, owned by him and two friends. He and his partners also owned two camps nearby, "Eagle's Nest" and "Johnny Leaf." He had said he looked forward to the time when he could live in the woods the year around, and one of the hardest parts of his affliction for him to bear was the limitation it put on his outdoor activities during the last few years.

Carolyn Malkin reported that her grandmother's last remembrance of her husband was that he said this: "Well, I've gotten myself in an awful mess, but I've had a hell of a time doing it."

Bob Gillespie heading up the Red Horse Trail on a winter day.

Part II

Harvey Dunham on
French Louie's Trail

Harvey Dunham at Wild Cat Cliff.

Chapter 18

Finding Louie

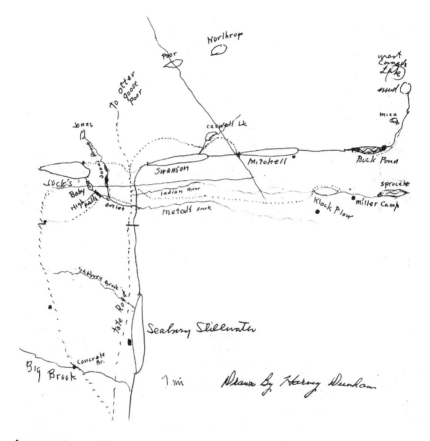

Northrup

Poor

to Otter
goose
poor

west
Conagh
Lake

mud

Jones

mica

Caswell Lk

Jock's
Baby
High falls
outlet

Swanson

Mitchell

Buck Pond

spruce lt

Indian River

Klock Plow

miller Camp

Metcalf brook

Seabury Brook

Tote Road

Seabury Stillwater

Big Brook

Concrete
Br.

7 mi

Drawn By Harvey Dunham

THAT HARVE KEPT BOB'S LETTERS for the rest of his life is a credit to everything Bob inspired in him. He was more than a friend and a partner; he was a teacher, a leader, and a mentor. "Segoolie!" Harve must have heard echoing from the grave, "Segoolie, Harve—carry on."

If Harve reread one of Bob's last letters, he would have heard Bob coaching from beyond. "I hope you won't quit writing for the *Outdoorsman*," he had written; "Your articles are the only good thing in it."

Harve did keep writing, submitting articles to magazines and keeping his camp journals up to date with visitor logs and camp adventures. And he added a new component to his notebooks: he began recording snippets of West Canada Country history, a rich folklore that was unfolding for him as a result of his unceasing curiosity.

By exploring all of the locally renowned points of interest in the vicinity of Fraser Clearing, Harve had become very knowledgeable of the region's topography. The maps he created promoting the camps demonstrate that, but he also reaped an unexpected bonus. Over the ten years since his first two-week stay at Trume Haskell's camp in 1924, Harve's excursions had brought him into contact with many local residents and camp owners who, once they were comfortable with him, began to share their personal and family histories. Legends leapt from the tongues of old-timers and the exploits of pioneer settlers were detailed by their descendants. The stories begged the interest of someone like Harve and he obliged, jotting down notes and sketching little maps. Inevitably, many of the tales necessitated further, in-person investigations—exactly the sort of backwoods outings that Harve loved to make. In this way Harve began learning about the region's founding characters, which added names and personality to the topography he had already cataloged in his head.

At Jocks Lake (now known as Honnedaga Lake) he learned that the host was a gambler named Amazia Dutton Barber who ran "Forest Lodge." When guests arrived, "Dut" might offer them a chance to wager their room rate "nothing or double," if they were so inclined.

Down in Wilmurt, Ed Wilkinson—whom everyone called "Uncle Ed"—ran the Wilmurt House. His place served as a general store and post office as well as a tavern and inn. Many tall tales first took flight from within those establishment's walls.

To get to Forest Lodge from Nobleboro back then you might've taken a buckboard drawn by one of "Big Eve's" teams stationed near Griff Evans' hotel, but by the time you got there you might have wish you'd walked. The road was said to be "uphill either way you travelled."

Harve heard about the Shepards, Conklins, Flansburgs, Becrafts and other prominent settler families. Some worked for Dut and others worked on the river drives, but the more Harve learned about the pioneer history of the Upper West Canada Valley, the more he realized that one man's activities seemed to permeate almost all of the mythology. The legends of many men had grown larger than life over time, but none as much as his. He was a lovable wild man that everybody knew about. Old men spoke of him with respect. He was a woodsman who lived by his wits and his toil in the wilderness during the last era when that could be done. He was the hermit whose domain stretched from Speculator to Forestport and Piseco to the Moose River Plains—the man everyone knew simply as "French Louie."

If all the stories were true, Louie Seymour had lived an intriguing life. He had been a lumberjack, a road monkey and a canal boat driver. He had run away with the circus and returned to become a woodsman and trapper. For the state Louie watched for fires. For his guests he guided fishing trips and hunts. When others dared not stay in the woods, Louie stayed there alone. On his few annual visits to civilization, Louie would announce his arrival with the howl of a wolf or the song of a loon and distribute candy or jerky to wide-eyed children who followed him on his way to the public house or tavern. Before long, the whole village knew that French Louie had come out of the woods. The barkeepers were especially happy when another of Louie's epic binges got under way.

Louis Seymour, widely known as "French Louie."

Harve was fascinated by Louie and since it seemed that every old-timer had his own French Louie story to tell, Harve decided that he would be the one to collect them all. The collection eventually became the foundation for a book about Louie, and Harve's singular legacy.

Peachy Barse first met Harve when he stayed at Trume Haskell's place in 1924. Peachy's dilapidated shack was just north of Fraser Clearing. As one of Harve's closest neighbors, Peachy was probably one of the first locals to a spin a few yarns about old French Louie.

Carolyn Malkin's prized photo of her grandfather sitting with Peachy Barse at Segoolie in August 1927.

Peachy was a retired lumberjack who had achieved some local fame by rescuing a fisherman from drowning in the rapids of West Canada Creek and later by pulling a man from a burning cabin. By the time Harve got to know him, Peachy was an old man, his existence becoming a hand-to-mouth affair. He still did a little hunting and fishing, but he survived mostly by serving as a caretaker for the camps owned by sportsmen who had christened their shanties with curious names such as the Woodpecker, Rochester, Red, Burnt Knoll, and Ralph Camps. Peachy watched over Harve's camps too.

Once Harve started seriously collecting stories about French Louie, Peachy not only shared his own recollections, but also provided insight about other old-timers who might have known Louie—and might still be around to talk about him. Armed with a list, Harve decided to try to find them all.

Isaac Kenwell was ninety-five when Harve found him. Old "Ike" had forty-five years worth of French Louie stories. They had looked out for each other while Ike was superintendent of a lumber camp on the Cedar River only a few miles away from Louie's Pillsbury Lake camp during the long winter of 1885. Ike's brothers, Wellington and Gerald, knew Louie too. Gerald wrote a nice article about Louie that was published in the *Conservationist* magazine in 1952, and later became part of a small book about Louie. "Small" may be an understatement. The book was tiny. It is shown here actual size.

When Harve located aging guide George Wandover, he drove him up to North Lake to see another old-timer, Wandover's old friend Byron Cool. When Cool got a gander at Wandover peering out the window of Harve's rickety auto, he shouted to his wife, "Ma . . . lookit what they got caged up here." Once they were reacquainted the old woodsmen recalled tales of by-gone days and old French Louie.

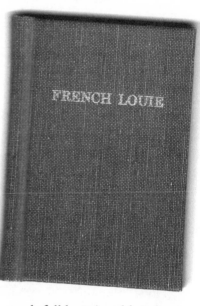

The day that Harve met the old lumber jobber Sol Carnahan, he may not have known that he had just struck folklorist's gold. Sol was one of the biggest jobbers to ever log the Upper West Canada Valley and he had been a personal friend of Louie's too.

Jobbers ran the show in the lumber business—bringing in everything necessary, the men, beasts, food and equipment to get the lumber to market—and Sol had been one of the most successful and well-liked jobbers in the region. There were two reasons for that. One, the land owners trusted Sol and two, Louie and the other lumberjacks thought of him as "one of them," a combination that brought Sol success.

When Harve began the interview, Sol told him he had ridden up the old "tote road" past Fraser Clearing more times than he could remember, but once he started recalling the old days of logging, a river of stories started pouring out.

Sol had started out as a lumberjack with his brothers, Ab and Irv, and made his Adirondack debut during the first Fourth of July there. A crowd had gathered on the bridge over the Black River at Bellingertown and the river was near flood stage. As the story was told, "Sol came, riding a spruce log in the mad water. The crowd cheered and Sol held his peavey, not crossways like an ordinary log driver, but straight up before him, and sailed beneath them under the bridge." From that day forward it was said that Sol "could ride a bubble if he had to." Sol first met Louie during those early days when they both worked the Southern Adirondack lumber camps.

Later on, when Sol became a jobber himself, he was able to hire the best "jacks" to work for him, because they knew they would get "better food and surer money" with Sol. They also respected that Sol had worked the peavey and saw, just like them. Sol had one other trait that his men loved. Sol knew when and how to throw his lumberjacks a party. One day, a piano at the Mansion House in Utica learned about Sol's parties the hard way. As Sol put it, "I always play with my feet." He bought a new piano for the owner of the Mansion House that day.

Not all the stories Harve heard from Sol were happy though. From Sol he learned that the life of a lumberman could be deadly. This fact was close to home for Sol.

The story was that about an hour before the big river drive of 1895, Sol's brother Ab was out on the river loosening logs when everyone suddenly heard a sound like the roar of the wind. But instead of wind it was water and Ab never had a chance. By mistake the dams had been tripped up-river an hour too soon. The massive rush of water came so fast and so hard that the log Ab was riding was thrown ten feet in the air. That was the last time anyone saw him alive. Louie was there later when they pried Ab's mutilated body loose from within the logjam, a third of a mile downstream.

Harve met another riverman, Truman Brown, at the recommendation of the bartender at the Union Hotel in Prospect. "The fellow you want to see is Truman Brown," the bar-keeper told him, "second house from the corner—lumberjack. He can tell you all about them days."

Truman did have quite a story to tell too. He had been working the same river drive as Ab Carnahan the day he was killed. Truman was almost killed the night before. He and a few other men were working a jam when another jam was dynamited upstream. The flood that came down chased Truman off the river, leaping from log to log. He jumped at the last possible second, grabbing onto the branches of a big birch tree, and swung to the ground just as the tree was uprooted by the surge. His survival allowed him the chance to settle down and marry. The result being that the two Trumes, Haskell and Brown, became brothers-in-law.

An unidentified riverman.

Jim Sturges knew Louie since he was a boy. He told Harve that he had trapped with Louie during the winter of 1879–80. He was sixteen years old at the time and had taken his dad's place at Louie's side that year. His father's name was Burr Sturges.

A fellow named "Pants" Lawrence had stories too. One was about a night he spent drinking with French Louie at the Brooks Hotel in "the Corners," now known as Speculator. That was the night before Louie died.

Ironically though, it ended up that one of the first people that Harve ever met in West Canada Country may have had the most French Louie stories of all. Harve and his friends had rented his cabin on their two-week visit to West Canada Creek back in 1924. His family had lived in that country for a couple of generations. Even the Chevarie Tote Road—as it had previously been known for the French lumber company Chevarie and Gendreu—had been renamed for his family. It was Haskell Road now and Trume Haskell, at one time, had been French Louie's best friend.

It took a little time to break the ice with Trume (as it had with several old-timers) but once Harve broke through there was a wealth of humor, adventure and information. Trume had done what few others could claim. He had lived with Louie, trapped with Louie, fished, hunted and laughed with Louie. Louie trusted Trume with many of his secrets. No other living person knew more about Louie's secret camps, hidden boats and food stashes than Trume Haskell.

Trume Haskell and Louie Seymour at Louie's camp. Enlargement from the photograph on the following page.

Had Trume not been such a good friend of Louie's, he might not have lived to tell about the day he killed four snakes at Louie's cabin while Louie was away. The snakes were Louie's pets. He had collected them from the woods and kept them around the camp to catch bugs in his garden and mice in his larder. After a long period of silence sitting with "the maddest Frenchman" Trume had ever seen, Louie finally spoke. "Wan ting nevaire do. Nevaire keel no more snake."

Harve enjoyed everything about the history he was gathering, the people he was meeting and the places he visited. His contributors seemed equally delighted that someone cared enough about their stories to write them down. Their memories of "the good old days" on West Canada Creek were important to them and they were pleased that they might be recorded for others to hear someday. Some interviewees may have inquired, "Harve, what do you plan to do with all this information?" Others may have been more direct: "So, when are you going to write a book?" But it didn't seem to matter to Harve. He was having too much fun collecting the folklore to worry. He loved his life at West Canada Creek and at that time, that was probably all that mattered.

Chapter 19
French Louie's Life at West Lake

Trume Haskell and Louie Seymour at Louie's camp on West Lake.

L IKE THE FOREST LANDS SURROUNDING Elmer Wilder's squatter's paradise, the forest domain of Louie Seymour was also primitive, storied and wild. Louie's was a diamond shape of wilderness roughly defined by the wagon trails that connected Atwell to Nobleboro to Newtons Corners (Speculator) and the Moose River Plains. Both regions had stands of virgin forest. Both had lakes and streams teaming with trout and salmon. Both were part of the original Totten and Crossfield Purchase of 1771, the first large-scale sale of land in the Adirondacks made by the British, and both were reclaimed by the State of New York and sold again after the American Revolution. Of course, who owned the land was somewhat irrelevant to Louie, just as it had been to Elmer. Louie was a squatter too and as long as he was free to enjoy the bounty of the land he was happy to put out fires and watch for lumber pirates.

Moving logs down a mountainside with sleds near Lewey Lake.

Louie arrived in the region in 1868, working at the lumber camps around Indian and Lewey Lakes. His first job was as a blacksmith's assistant, but he soon had an ax in hand. Louie liked to chop, but Louie, like most lumberjacks, was a "jack of all trades." Good lumberjacks had to be, because each season demanded different types of work. Summer was the time for chopping; in fall, new camps, haul roads and landings had to be built; during winter, the roads had to be iced and maintained in order to get as many logs to the rivers as possible; and when spring came—a time of waiting, excitement and danger for the lumberjacks—Mother Nature alone determined when the logging season would end—when the ice finally melted and the log drive began.

Louie made a name for himself as a river-driver that spring, and walked out of the woods with his pay for the entire year. It didn't last long, though. As Gerald Kenwell put it, "He liked his fling when outside." He wasn't alone either. It was like that for a lot of lumberjacks.

Louie worked the lumber camps until 1873, when he decided to see if he could make a living hunting and trapping. He threw up a small camp in the shadows of Snowy Mountain and from there he slowly worked his way farther into the wilderness, setting up trapping camps,

Heavy cables kept the sleds from kareening down the steep slopes.

cave shelters and cubby holes throughout the region. He built at the Jessup River and Cedar Lakes and eventually ended up at Pillsbury Lake, where he built two sturdy lean-tos facing each other.

In 1878, Louie partnered up with Burr Sturges, one of the most respected trappers in Newton Corners, using Burr's "slab shanty" on West Lake as a headquarters. Burr explained that his brother Chet had built the cabin on the same location where he had discovered evidence of a much older camp in 1850. Chet liked the little clearing and decided to build there. Louie liked it too; the following year, after trapping the season with Burr's son Jim, he spruced up the shanty and moved in permanently. He expanded the clearing, brought in some chickens and started a garden.

The soil was not good, but with spring suckers plentiful, Louie enriched the ground by using them as fertilizer, sometimes placing a whole fish under each potato mound. In later years, Louie's potatoes and the army of snakes he employed as their guardians would become the stuff of legends.

Louie started work on a new cabin around 1885. From then on he called it home.

The clearing on West Lake was a remarkably beautiful location.[14] From the water's edge, the full length of West Lake stretched across a crystal mile to the northwest, with enormous chiseled erratics decorating the north and south shores. The scene was bordered by majestic, unnamed mountains rising in the distance.

Louie's cabin on West Lake.

The rugged lay of the land surrounding West Lake had held most settlers at bay during the years leading up to Louie's arrival. As in most pioneer developments, the rivers were the highways, so their headwaters were usually the last places settled. The West Canadas were at the top of not one, but two watersheds, making the region particularly remote. Brook Trout Lake drained west through the Indian River; Mud Lake emptied south via West Canada Creek.

But the slow and steady march of the lumber trade was making its way closer to Louie. In 1890, Johnny Leaf, built a hunting camp at the outlet of Mud Lake from which he planned to supply venison to the encroaching lumber camps for "from three to ten dollars per deer." Louie was not fond of the idea of having a neighbor so close by, especially Johnny Leaf. During a previous run-in with Leaf at Osborn's Adirondack House in Newtons Corners, Louie had accused Johnny of stealing his traps. Johnny had lunged at Louie with a knife and Louie had hit Johnny with a spittoon, its putrid contents spilling all over Johnny's face. If not for the intrusion of bystanders there, one of them might not have survived that night. Later, after Johnny had been supplying venison for the lumber camps for a while, and making lots of threats about Louie to anyone who'd listen, Louie finally met Johnny in the woods face to face. Louie asked him straight out, "You gonna keel me Johnny?"

"No Louie, no. Ba goshy, yo' s'pose a man's gonna keel off hees' bes' fren?"

14 West Lake is the largest of the lakes collectively known as the West Canada lakes. During the 1800s West Lake was also known by the names Big West and North Lake. It is also mistakenly called West Canada Lake. For the rest of this book we will refer to it as West Lake.

View of West Lake from the shore behind Louie's cabin.

For the time at least, the woods was big enough for both of them and it must have seemed smarter that day to have a friend so far from civilization, rather than an enemy.

After exiting Mud Lake, West Canada Creek carved south through four miles of boulder-strewn rapids until it slowed again in a series of three natural stillwaters. By the fall of 1890, Joe Mitchell of Indian Lake had constructed a dam at the foot of the Second Stillwater and Charley Swanson had one at the first as the loggers crept farther up the valley.[15]

The following fall the lumbermen reached Louie when a dam was constructed right next to Johnny Leaf's camp at the Mud Lake Outlet. Louie's wilderness domain was shrinking, but in the end, that was not so bad for him.

The Adirondack League Club had bought Barber's Forest Lodge, as well as the Bisby Lodge and the Mountain Lodge and every other lodge within the 104,000 acres they had purchased in 1890. Dut Barber remained in charge at Forest Lodge and they even set up a post office there with Dut as the first postmaster. When Webb's railroad started running they built a station between the Remsen and Forestport Stations and called it Honnedaga. The Adirondacks were becoming popular and money was flowing into the woods. New camps were being built as big-city sportsmen sought adventure. Louie's place at West Lake became a popular destination for the hardiest sports.

---

[15] The two stillwaters still retain the Mitchell and Swanson names.

Things were busy for the next few years. Logging continued, the League Club prospered and Louie's guiding business ran steady until July of 1898, when the Adirondack League Club acquired Moose River Tract Township Number 8 and part of Number 7. The 22,000-acre acquisition included the section of West Canada Creek that ran from the rapids below the first stillwater all the way up to Mud Lake. The membership, being afraid that further logging would hurt the trout population, decided to blow the

The Swanson Dam.

Mitchell and Swanson Dams. They also decided to remove all squatters and tear down all unnecessary structures. That included every logging camp except the one at the Swanson, Johnny Leaf's shanty too. It was burned down and Johnny was put off the land. Johnny responded by saying "de likker, she too far." He moved 25 miles downstream, to an abandoned camp at Fraser Clearing on the Seabury Stillwater.

The League Club couldn't put Louie out of his camp at West Lake though; they didn't own that far up. But there had been opposition to Louie building a camp there years before. That ended quickly when the owners heard Louie remark, "Ah used to put out a lot o' fire. Now ah guess maybe ah let 'em burn."

Once the logging companies were gone, nature reclaimed the camps and open spaces quickly. Deer flourished on the low browse growing in the clearings left behind after trees had been removed and the far-away feeling of remoteness that had left West Lake for a time returned to Louie's abode. With game abundant, an incredible

The Mitchell Stillwater.

lakeside vista and a true north-country character as proprietor, Louie's guiding and hosting business became more popular than ever.

To facilitate his growing clientele, Louie decided to build a log hotel at the clearing, the biggest of all the cabins he had ever built. He began sometime in 1914 by collecting the perfect stones for a large fireplace around which he would construct the building. He found stones along the lakeshore and brought them over with his boat. Whenever his friend Perkins was in with his mules, Louie had him drag the larger stones on a "stone-boat" Louie had made. The largest capping stone was drawn to camp that way. When the lake froze that winter, Louie dragged many over on a sled. Slowly, toiling alone with a homemade tripod and tackle, Louie carefully laid up each stone, the aches and pains in his approximately eighty-year-old body making the work all the harder.

On February 25, 1915, Louie went ice fishing. He wasn't feeling well, but he had decided to head out to the Corners and he wanted to take some trout with him for Mrs. Brooks at the Brooks Hotel. He caught four nice ones, plenty enough. The next morning he strapped on his snowshoes and headed out early. With short strides and long breaths he made it to his Pillsbury Lake Camp, started a warming fire and stayed the night.

If Louie spent some time reminiscing that night, halfway back to the Corners, he had a lot to remember. Nights when he would arrive at the bar with a pack full of furs, slapping down a mink skin as tender and shouting "a drink for the bar!" He rarely got change. Or a childhood memory, working as a mule-driver on the Erie Canal towpath when he was only twelve, when he developed some of his blood-curdling animal imitations in order to keep the panthers thinking twice about having young Louie for dinner. And the amazing circus years, the sounds and colors and smells he remembered from days travelling with those crazy shows. The river drives, living on pure adrenaline inches from death. Many lumberjacks had not been as lucky or as good as French Louie. There was so much to remember as he drifted to sleep.

The next day, when Louie howled his arrival at the Corners it was not as powerful as it once had been, but nonetheless everyone nearby knew, Louie was back in town. It was Friday at the Brooks Hotel. He dropped his pack and slid down into a chair. "Ba Cripe," he sighed. He was happy to be there. After a little rest he unpacked the trout for an excited Mrs. Brooks, said "hallou" to the familiar faces at the bar and sat down for a drink. A warm feeling spread from his head to his toes. "Ba da holy feesh. Louie, da boy!"

"French Louie"
Seymour

Louie died there that night. Pants Lawrence, who was drinking with him, said, "looks as if I bought him the last slug of whiskey he'll ever gargle."

Ernest Brooks, the proprietor of the hotel, said he'd pay for the casket. He wanted Louie to have a "decent funeral."

Jim "Pants" Lawrence.

Harve Dunham later wrote that "The Corners felt it," because "Louie had belonged to them."

The stories about Louie after his death read more like folktales than eulogies. This one ran in the *Gloversville Morning Herald.*

Aged Adirondack Guide Dead at Speculator

Some Interesting Stories and Reminiscences of Louis Seymour's Life Spent Close to Nature's Heart in the North Woods.

Louis Seymour, aged between seventy-five and eighty years, and better known as "French Louie," died of Bright's disease at Brooks Hotel at Speculator, Saturday afternoon about 4 o'clock. The deceased was making one of his periodical visits to "The Corners," as Speculator is known to those residing in that vicinity, when he was taken ill. The disease had reached the advanced stages and his entire system had become saturated with the poison, skilled measures having been ineffectual in staying the progress of the disease, rugged as was the constitution of the deceased.

"French Louie" was one of the best known and most popular trappers and guides of the lower Adirondacks. For more than forty years of his lifetime he had been located at or in the vicinity of Speculator. He plied his trade on the West Canada and its tributaries and at Cedar Lake. He lived alone and for all this long term of years he had made a living by trapping, hunting and guiding. Many sportsmen in Gloversville, Johnstown and Amsterdam will recall "French Louie" especially well, while there are scores further removed who have followed the lead of the aged guide, who even in his later years was able to tire the best of the younger men who he guided to the sleeping places of the trout or the runways of the deer.

Just how old "French Louie" was no one ever knew, nor did any of his associates ever know who his parents were. He was known to be a French-Canadian. He was of a diffident nature and not in the habit of talking about himself. Those who knew him well estimate his age at being 74. He went to Lewey Lake in the early seventies from Canada. One season he had traveled with a circus. However, the call of the wild rang louder to "Louie" than did the lure of the "big top." A hunter and woodsman by birth and instinct he forsook the sawdust arena and the crash of the band, forswore the glamour of the circus forever to spend his days in the woods and to live nearer nature's heart.

In the year 1873 he made his first appearance at Lewey Lake. He built a small hut. During the winter he captured two deer alive, built a small pen and fed the animals on shin hemlock [American yew,] a diet of which the captives were much fond. Later the deer were sold to the owner of a park in Saratoga. He did not remain long at Lewey Lake—perhaps one season. The influx of visitors during the summer disturbed him. He loved the solitude; he cared not much for his fellow men. Next he moved to Pillsbury Lake, twelve miles from Speculator. Here he cleared off the lumber and raised potatoes and some vegetables. He established camps at West Lake, Pillsbury Lake and Otter Brook.

He spent most of his time at the latter camp where he acted as guide for summer campers. The latter camp was accessible to Cedar Lake, Whitney and Sampson Lakes. For two years he was a partner of James Sturges, the well known northern guide. The two had a chain of traps extending from West Canada to Jocks Lake on the south and to Moose River on the north. The line covered eighteen miles and the inspection trip required two days. Many valuable furs were taken each winter, including such fur as marten, which in those days were plentiful; the price ranged per skin from $1.50 upwards. The present price is $8 [in 1915]. Other furs taken were fisher, mink, and bear.

Among his business enterprises was that of making maple sugar. There was an abundance of maple trees in the vicinity. "Louie" built a sugar house of rough material which he dragged to the vicinity on wood shod sleds, and built a fire box of rough stone. He made his buckets of birch bark. The buckets were collapsible ones, ingeniously made. The bottom was cleverly folded and secured by a birch skewer so firmly that not a drop of the sap could filter through. It required much skill in emptying the buckets, but "Louie" was adept in this art, and his proficiency in this line was marveled at by all who witnessed his work.

A resident of this city who yearly visited the northern country tells an interesting reminiscence of "Louie" which happened some years ago. The visitor, who was seated in front of "Louie's" domicile in conversation with the woodsman, became startled at the sight of a large snake approaching from the nearby woodpile. He stopped and picked up a club. "Louie," noting the action, sprang to the side of the visitor and seizing his arm asked, "What are you going to do? "I'm going to kill that snake," was the answer.

"Don't molest him," said "Louie."

"That's 'Darby.' He won't harm you. Look, here comes 'Joan.' Those snakes help me in my work. They have lived with me all winter. They clean up the meat block and in the summer keep the potato vines free of potato bugs."

"Louie's" claims were true. The snakes shared his domicile with him, and were his only farm hands. They cleaned the slaughter block free of all fragments which might accumulate and also ate all the potato bugs which appeared on the vines. He allowed no one to harm the snakes and in return the reptiles labored faithfully as any farm hand for their board and keep. He shared his provender with "Joan" and "Darby" until the end of their natural life.

"Louie" in his northern solitudes did not know the day of the week, nor cared naught what day it was. He cared naught for gold. All he cared for was to live the life of his forefathers—to live the life he had chosen in his own way—far from the madding crowd—free from the carking care and the petty jealousy of so-called civilized man.

The waters nearby abounded with the finest specimens of the finny tribe. He was an expert fisherman—never using a pole or rod in trout fishing, he spurned the elaborate fly book of the amateur trout fisher. A line and hook and the consummate skill of the woodsman sufficed him to capture all the trout he wished.

"French Louie" was slight of build, weighing less than 150 pounds, and was about five foot, eight inches, but of wondrous strength. His law was that of "Squatter sovereignty." Although he had possession of the land on which he lived merely by tolerance of the owner, nevertheless he resented the appearance of any intruder in his section.

"Louie" was sensitive to injury or ill treatment and highly appreciative of kind treatment. He loved his friends warmly and was ever loyal to them, but he never forgot any injury done him. He cared nothing for the outside world, nothing for politics, never discussed creeds, but was honest and believed in the gospel of hard work. Woodcraft was his one aim in life. He has passed on to a happier hunting ground and will be long recalled in loving remembrance by many men prominent in the clergy, in the professions and in business life in this immediate section, who shared his hospitality in the years gone by.

They say that school was closed in Speculator the day they buried French Louie. Before the casket was closed, children filed by and laid sprigs of balsam on the body. Ernest Brooks followed through on his promise and paid for the casket. Louie was indeed given a proper send off. But there wasn't any money for a headstone. Loose dirt was all that marked the last resting place of Speculator's favorite hermit.

Chapter 20
Saving Louie's Fireplace

I F LOUIE SEYMOUR HAD ANY LIVING RELATIVES, no one in Speculator knew of them and none ever came forward, so on July 7, 1915, when George Wilson leased the camp at West Lake from the Union Bag and Paper Company for one dollar "payable yearly," he also inherited everything that Louie left behind.

The *Amsterdam Recorder's* "Man about town" reported in 1917 that "being a blacksmith by trade and also a handyman with the carpenter's tools, [Mr. Wilson] soon fixed it up and made it a most attractive place, kept scrupulously clean . . . men who like good fishing go in there and enjoy excellent sport."

Though he made improvements to the cabin, George Wilson never disturbed Louie's fireplace. He left it alone—a memento to Louie.

Twelve years later (in 1927) the state acquired the land from Union Bag and Paper and told Wilson he had to go. Wilson removed everything that he could haul out and burned the camp to the ground. When he was gone, all that remained was Louie's fireplace.

The ranger station contructed at West Lake after Louie's cabin was burned down.

The state decided to utilize the clearing in 1929, and a small log cabin was erected there as a station house. Forest Ranger Ernest Ovitt was selected as the man to run the station because of his familiarity with the country from his days in the lumber business back in the 1920s. David Beetle wrote about Ovitt in his book *West Canada Creek:*

> Ernest Ovitt ... New York's most hard-to-get-at ranger.
> If he's not fighting fires, "Ernie"—that's what he likes to be called—keeps busy.
>
> He keeps some 35 miles of trail clear (and mowed out too. . . .)
>
> He maintains fresh spruce-bough beds in four or five state leantos.
>
> He puts bridges back as fast as the streams sweep them away.
>
> He plays St. Bernard to lost or ailing campers.
>
> He gives advice—when asked—on how to cook brook trout, what the weather's going to be, which trail is shorter, what to do for black fly bites, where's the best place to see deer, or which spoon will be most likely to snare a lake trout. . . .
>
> His "register book" lists only about 50-75 persons a year, and while he misses a good many while out clearing the trails, he doesn't believe the traffic load would more than double those figures.

After nine years there, Ernie outgrew the cabin and the state developed plans to demolish it so that a larger one could be built in its place. Along with the cabin, Louie's fireplace was scheduled to be dismantled, and the stones used in the foundation of the new station.

When the news reached Harve Dunham, who had become locally known as a collector of French Louie's history, he instinctively converted from historian to defender. The fireplace was the last relic of Louie's legacy and he saw no reason to destroy it. Harve went public with his opposition to the state's plans in letters and with this opinion piece, which appeared in the *Utica Observer-Dispatch* on September 26, 1938:

Utican Urges Old Landmark Be Preserved

Plan to Destroy Chimney Built by Hermit Is Protested

A petition to the State Conservation Department not to tear down an old stone fireplace built by French Louie at the West Canada Lakes was contemplated today by Harvey L. Dunham, Utica.

The state is about to build quarters for a ranger at the lakes and plans to use the stone from the fireplace for the foundation. This would erase the last vestige of the hermit who lived at the lakes for 10 years, said Mr. Dunham, and would destroy what amounts to a monument built by a man who has become a legendary character of the region.

Dunham recalled that the late Charles A. Gianini, Poland, in a page-long story of the West Canada Creek published in a Sunday edition of the *Utica Observer-Dispatch* some years ago, predicted that the fireplace would remain many years as a reminder of the old trapper and woods inhabitant.

Louie built the fireplace intending to erect a larger camp, but died at an old age before completing the task, said Mr. Dunham. There are two small buildings at the campsite which the state will tear down. Mr. Dunham said there are plenty of stones about the shore of the lake that could be used for the foundation for the ranger's quarters.

The West Canada Lakes are reached by a good trail and sometimes by airplane. Mr. Dunham yesterday walked in to the lakes to inspect the site and came back out the same day. The West Canada Lakes are in one of the most remote sections of the Adirondacks and are visited afoot only by the most hardy. The state is carrying in by airplane some of its equipment for the construction of the ranger camp, said Mr. Dunham. He encourages anyone interested in the Adirondacks to write, asking the Conservation Department to preserve the relic of the hermit.

The clearing and fireplace as it looked in 2010.

Harve's appeal immediately struck a nerve. Citizens and sportsmen's groups responded quickly, writing not only to the Conservation Commission, but also to politicians and newspapers. The clamor caused the department to back down by the end of October and a letter was sent to Harve assuring him that the fireplace would be left alone. Construction of the new cabin ended up on hold until 1950, when the old cabin was finally destroyed and a new one built without harming Louie's fireplace. Since then, the site has been visited by thousands of hikers and remains a popular destination for modern fans of *Adirondack French Louie*.

Chapter 21
A Woodsman's Hobby

At the foot of Buck Pond Stillwater.

ALL THROUGH THE 1930S AND '40S, Harve continued his quest for information about French Louie and the history of the Upper West Canada Valley. Exploration was always a key component of his pursuit and an endeavor that tested his skills of navigation, observation, survival and woodcraft. It was both a passion and a sport, a hobby that pleased him, and he allowed the information he gathered to direct his expeditions to wherever they led him.

Energized by the description of some interesting place that an old-timer had shared, Harve would set a date, send out invitations, ready his gear and plan a menu. One such trip was an investigation of the area half-way between Segoolie and the West Canada Lakes, beyond the rapids above the second stillwater to a placid stretch of river called Buck Pond. On this particular trip Harve, his brother and a few friends, would be looking for several of Sol Carnahan's old logging camp clearings as well as some fishing holes that Harve presumed to be along Louie's old trapline.

When bushwhacking off-trail, Harve was always on the lookout for old blazes cut into consecutive trees, the grown-over slashes, arrows, or letters carved into the bark that indicated that a trail had once been marked there. He would also watch out for the remains of earlier activity—small clearings, chains embedded in the limbs of a tree, or the neck of a bottle poking out of the ground that might be on top of an old trash heap—any of which might lead to the discovery of a ruined dwelling. His woods detective work provided the ultimate treat when any real treasure was uncovered.

From Bob Gillespie's example, set long ago, Harve recorded many of his activities, jotting down in a field book or his camp log the highlights of the trip, trail conditions, streams crossed, fishing results and any interesting sightings of flora and fauna. Sometimes he sketched a map.

The following is one such account, an eight-day trip that Harve made with his brother Ray, Harvey Broughton and Frank Devecis to Buck Pond Stillwater, up into French Louie Country in 1938. Frank Devecis later illustrated Harve's book about French Louie.

A Frank Devecis charicature of Harve in search of firewood, 1946.

The Trip to Buck Pond

Summer, 1938
Written by Harve and Ray Dunham

Harve or Frank Devecis drew this to commemorate their trip to Buck Pond in 1937. It shows a similar view to the one in the photograph on page 211.

In the evening at Segoolie, we worked on arranging our grub and put what we could in cardboard containers, labeling them and fastening the covers with adhesive tape, and then we checked the list and discussed further lightening. The Karo syrup is questioned. It weighs a pound and a half. It's heavy. "Cut it out. Instead add more sugar," someone says.

"All right, cut it out."

"I say you got too much flour, cut out a pound."

"All right then cut out a pound of that Swedish bread. I don't like it anyway."

"Nothing doing, we need it but we don't need the flour."

"You agree to cut out the bread and I'll cut out the flour."

"All right cut'em out. You got too much dried beef anyway so cut out this can of corn beef."

"How about leaving one of these split peas to camp?"

"No, I like my pea soup."

"Well then here's what we are cutting out: 1 lb. of flour, 1 loaf of Swedish bread, 1 can of Karo and 1 can of corn beef."

"Do we need the water pail?"

"It only weighs a pound. Sure we need it."

"We can get along without it."

"We can get along without a lot of things but we don't want to. We will have a lot of trout."

"How about leaving the pail at camp and taking another frying pan?"

The packs are made up and weighed with everything in including sleeping pads. They averaged 49 lbs. 4 men, 8 days.

The Start

The packs were weighed in the evening as we made them up and again the next morning as we were leaving. Frank went up the trail with us as far as the Woodpecker Camp cable crossing, where he began fishing as we shouldered our packs, waved "so long" and started up the hogs back on the other side up the Indian a short distance past Buck Run, following the old tote road up the mountain. We rested several times on the climb and soon were over the top swinging down the easier grade towards Sol Carnahan's # 2, where we stopped and drank from the little brook that crosses the trail there.[16]

Hunting Camp

Near Klock Flow, before you get to Twin Rock outlet we stopped to look over the old hunting camps which used to be used by the [Ed] Richards party from Herkimer. It is a log camp with gable ends about 8 x 12 without a roof, as they brought in canvas to use as a roof.

---

[16] Sol Carnahan was a lumberman who ran several logging camps identified by numbers in the vicinity of West Canada Creek. Sol shared many stories with Harve and described to him the locations of several of his abandoned camps.

Klock Flow on the Indian River.

It had gable ends, almost 4 logs high on the sides with a door at the end. There was a good stove in it protected from the weather by a few boards. There was also a large oil drum lying on its side which had been fitted with a cover to keep food stuff in it. We kicked it to see if it was full and through a hole on the edge of the cover a very neat and clean woods-mouse stuck his head out and looked around to see what was going on. Before we got through kicking the barrel, fifteen slick and well groomed mice came out one at a time to see what the big idea was. They don't look like house mice.

Section Pieces
Miller Camp, Sol Carnahan's #3

Moving on again we crossed Twin Rock outlet and bearing to the right around Klock Flow. Then we could hear the Indian to our left and a few hundred feet further came to the old Miller Camp. At the old Miller Camp we stopped for lunch, a drink of Klim [powdered milk], some Triscuits, cheese, dried beef, and candy. The punkies bothered us

The Indian River near the ford to Miller Camp.

some while eating so we built a smudge fire of rotten wood. The Miller Camp is nothing more than a grassy opening in the woods on the Indian River just above the Klock Flow. It was originally a lumber camp. I think [it was] Klock's before it became Sol Carnahan's #3. Then the Adirondack League Club got it and used it for awhile for an outlying camp for their members but there was not enough there to attract them and they didn't use it, but as everyone else did, the League burned it down. Today apparently there is nothing there but grass, but if one pokes around as we did after we had eaten lunch, many reminders are found of the old days. There are old stoves a plenty, bottles galore—not all whiskey bottles either, as we found two marked with embossed letters that read "gargle oil," old iron, chains, bolts, sleigh runners and six broken cross cut saws. Raymond found an axe head which seemed as he tested it on a rock to still have its temper. He put it in his pack. Shined up with a new helve in it, it will be around Segoolie for years to come.

We left a note here for Frank, displayed in a bottle on a stick surrounded by an array of whiskey and gargle oil bottles saying that all's okay and we were!

Crossing the Indian River on the rocks just above the Miller camp, a quarter of a mile or so through the woods on the north side of the Indian, we came to Belden Vly Creek, where the party camped in 1929. Before following the creek, I tried to locate just what route I had taken nine years before, but something was amiss. We left Belden Vly creek before we came to the vly and turned up a steep notch toward the north.

The Campsite

We did not want to camp at the old campsite at the head of the rifts, so we scouted around on both sides of the creek at the foot of the flow and picked a place just above the old site on high ground facing the east directly up the stillwater. It was a small clearing about 50 x 75 feet made years before, apparently by beaver felling several birch trees. The beaver no doubt used the small limbs on these trees. The heavy trunks still lay there. One large stump was right in front of the tent back of where we built our fire with the down trunk of the tree still connected to it. We cut them in 4 to 8 foot lengths. They were heavy and hard and all we could lift but fared good in our night fires. We unearthed an iron oar lock which had probably laid there for many years. This country was active with logging around 1900–1910.

The old peavey head that Frank and I found the previous year was still there and will be for years to come as no one would want to carry weight bad enough to take it out. We pitched our tent with good sized logs on the sides and back, making the tent off the ground and much roomier. We carried rocks from the creek and made a fireplace. The tent, put up with crotches and a log pole, faced the rising sun. Harvey B. could open his eyes in the morning without rising in his bed and look up the stillwater at the sunrise back of the spruces and the heavy white mists rolling up off the water. The hard outside shell of a dead stub furnished us with board like material with which we made a table to keep our tinware on and to use just as a handy place to sit things down when cooking and eating.

The Rafts

Making our rafts was not such a hard job. It took us four hours to make two. Raymond and Harvey B. got into the water. The water was cold.

Just below our camp, about a hundred feet from the foot of the stillwater where we crossed in the rifts were enough old dead standing balsams to supply us with the basic building material. We cut out an opening in the alders and carried the logs to the shore. The dead balsam trees were dry and dead and the logs were not heavy. Each raft required 5 logs about 12 feet long. Four green spruce poles (one for each end) were cut, notched, laid across to span the width, and then spiked into the 12 foot logs with spikes. The larger longer logs were made into a two man raft; the other was lighter, for one man, which was mine. They securely bound the logs together. Ray and Harvey B. did the nailing in about 3 feet of water. For a space of 5 or 6 feet on the logs we laid thick evergreen boughs. They were very buoyant and moved easily. Toward the end of the week they began to settle.

Birds

Anyone who loves birds would be right in their element upon the Buck Pond Stillwater. As we cleaned up around camp Harvey B. would be singing or whistling and the many small birds of all colors would all be singing, joining in with Harvey, and when we would stop they would stop. We noticed it another time when Harvey was whistling; when he stopped the woods would be quiet. There were not many ducks on the stillwater. Now and then one or two would go over us and as they did would look down on us on our raft. In the alders at the water's edge and on one high dead treetop of a live spruce near the Stillwater, large woodpeckers would perch and cry down at us as Harvey B. yelled a warning, "Keep your hat on!" One lone sea gull went past everyday and once we heard a low, swish, swish of wings and looked up as a great blue heron flew over. Hawks circled over us with a large wingspan and another small, like a sparrow hawk. I saw swallows and other small birds chasing the smaller hawks.

In an Indian River bend on the way over there was a very neat and symmetrical bird's nest with 4 eggs in it.

The view from the head of Buck Pond Stillwater.

Fishing

Trying to fish from the shore of Buck Pond Stillwater is terrible, but from a raft on the water there isn't anything better. It's a wonderful spot. In places it is eight to twelve feet deep and fifty to a hundred feet wide. Around the bends it is about a mile long, narrowing toward the head. The shore is overhanging alders back of which is heavy spruce, and a few low mountains and a sky and clouds which too seem to belong distinctly to this North Country. The place is wild and beautiful and perhaps—although we didn't find it out—perhaps it is full of trout, who knows? It is a good place for trout to live. The water is cold and the bottom is hard. The fishing was disappointing. It might have been the weather. One day we caught between 25 and 30 fish, 10 of them on flies. The largest one was 13 inches and caught on a worm. Other days ran poor. They would not rise to a fly. Ray and Harvey B. covered the stillwater thoroughly several times, one poling and the other fly casting. There are two sharp bends on the stillwater which appeared to be the best places to fish where we anchored our rafts and enjoyed the scenery if not the fish.

One day we fished the rifts down as far as the head of the Mitchell but only got about a half dozen keepers. But we had what fish we wanted to eat. Some meals we ate 12 or 15, which was not as many as we fried. They tasted good, fried and eaten when they were really fresh.

What We Learned

After the trip we decided a few changes would be better. Take one lb. more sugar as this was the only thing we were really a little low on. Two pounds of dried peas was OK although we did have one left. It's good stuff. No more pumpernickel. That's out. It doesn't go. Take along a folding aluminum reflector oven and take along another pound each of flour and corn meal for Johnny cakes. Take along a small bottle of vanilla for rice pudding. Three pounds of Klim [powdered milk] is OK although I think that one can of heavy condensed milk might be added for coffee which would make more Klim for oatmeal and drinking and cooking. I would say to take the next larger size of baking powder. The rest of the list was perfect.

Harve, his guests and friends made many such trips over the years and though they didn't always find what they were looking for, the Upper West Canada Valley always proved to be an exhilarating region to explore.

Chapter 22

The Forever Wild Debate
Rekindled

URING THE LATE 1940S, Harve took up his pen again and
teamed up with other conservation-minded individuals to
advocate for a cause that was as close to his heart as French
Louie—a cause as important to him as the West Canada Country
itself.

Toward the end of nineteenth century, at the height of New York's
river log drives and canal boat commerce, nearly every good location
for a dam in the Adirondacks had been used. Some dams were temporary, opened up each spring to move logs down river, while others
had been built and re-built, ever higher, to provide flood control and a
steady flow of water to the canal system. But there were two locations
on the Moose River just south of the Fulton Chain where dams had
been planned that were never built—at Higley Mountain and Panther
Mountain. As World War II came to an end, plans for the two projects were dusted off and resurrected. In the process, the debate over
the public's interpretation of "forever wild" as it related to the Forest
Preserve was re-kindled. The political battles that ensued took over a
decade to resolve and included two referendums to amend the State
Constitution before they came to an end.

The problem was that both dams and their flood zones were entirely
within the "Blue Line," and the larger Panther Mountain Dam would
not only flood some 1,500 acres of Forest Preserve, but would also
result in the taking of 3,400 acres of private property belonging to
the Adirondack League Club. The club's leadership was completely
opposed to the idea, which meant the land would have to be taken
from them through eminent domain, virtually insuring a protracted
legal fight.

Advocates of the dam projects argued that they were necessary in order to prevent flooding, improve Watertown's municipal water supply, and provide additional hydroelectric power. Opponents countered with a long list of rebuttals, but the most compelling encompassed an idea bigger than opposition to the projects themselves. Building the dams would establish precedents that threatened to terminally alter the definition of "forever wild." If both Forest Preserve land and private property were allowed to be taken for dams that would be in part used for commercial purposes, how many more hydro-electric projects would soon follow? The State Constitution had been amended explicitly to say "The lands of the State . . . constituting the forest preserve . . . shall be forever kept as wild forest lands. They shall not be leased, sold, or exchanged, or be taken by any corporation, public or private, nor should the timber thereon be sold, removed, or destroyed." Wouldn't Adirondack League Club land be taken? Wouldn't timber be destroyed by flooding new reservoirs? What about the buildings, roads and power lines—were they all of a conforming use?

The arguments, both for and against, were focused directly to the court of public opinion, because the debate would have to be settled at the ballot box, just as it had been in 1894. Without changing the constitution the dams were unlikely to be built, so the core question for the people of New York would be: do you support the 1894 forever wild amendment or not?

In 1947, Governor Dewey halted the Higley dam project, but threw his full support behind the larger reservoir at Panther Mountain. As the debate heated up, it became known that the level of the water in the Panther Mountain Reservoir might vary as much as 125 feet. That was when Harve Dunham decided to contribute his voice to the chorus of opinions opposed to the dam. He wrote to the *Utica Daily Press* in October 1949:

> Those who are interested in keeping the Adirondacks wild should not be thrown off their trail by the misleading editorial which appeared in the *Utica Daily Press* under the title of "It's Ours, Let's Use It," about the Panther Mountain dam.

Fifty to 75 years ago the lumbermen all over the woods were
building dams for water storage to float out their logs. When the
lumbering was over the trees on the shoreline were killed and a new
shoreline created. Taking out these dams and lowering the water level
would certainly not give the lakes their original appearance so the
dams were kept in condition and the lakes eventually regained their
beautiful shoreline.

Is this any argument why the lumbermen or any other despoilers
of the woods should be allowed to go right on building dams, even
though in 50 to 75 years nature does pretty well in covering up the
damage?

It is true that the woods are not as wild as they were; one couldn't
expect that. But we should fight to do what we can to save the bit
of wilderness that we have and keep the Adirondack Park as wild as
possible for our children and those to come.

In the midst of the legal maneuvering and debate over the Panther
Mountain dam, a devastating act of nature caused another, possibly
greater threat to the Forest Preserve. In November 1950, a massive storm
smashed through the Adirondack Park with hurricane-force winds that
struck from the opposite direction of those that normally prevailed.
The result was nearly a million acres of damaged forest, approximately
420,000 acres of which "sustained a blow-down loss of between 25 and
100 per cent" according to then Conservation Commissioner Perry
B. Duryea. Mature open forests were instantly turned into impassible
tumbles of toppled trees and the destructive storm soon became known
simply as the "big blow-down."

The threat to the preserve came when the State Conservation
Commission wrote to the Attorney General seeking authority to cir-
cumvent the constitution and hire lumber companies to salvage the
fallen timber. The rationale was to prevent forest fires, but the argument
was clouded by the motivations of profit. It may have been legal to
remove the fallen timber, but was it legal to sell it?

While the Attorney General was researching his opinion, voices in
the lumber industry that had long been silenced by the forever wild

amendment were suddenly vocal in their desire to help protect the Adirondacks—by removing all the freshly fallen trees. Hunters chimed in with support for the idea too, suggesting that logging would create new browsing areas for deer and other game.

Less than a month after the storm, but before the opinion was announced, Harve shared his opinion of the situation with an editorial in defense of "forever wild." He wrote:

> Recent articles and editorials in the *Utica Daily Press* about the trees blown down by the "big wind" of Nov. 25 seem to lament the fact that the trees must lie where they fall, eventually to rot. That's nothing to worry about.
>
> The small evergreens and hard woods (not "weed trees") are already there, the fallen trees have not disturbed them and the light being let in, these small trees will now grow fast and soon fill up the gap. It's not like a fire where all the young trees are killed.
>
> Tractors and mechanical equipment would kill the young trees and do many times more damage than the value of what little timber they could salvage. In most Adirondack areas lumbermen have to be very choosy in cutting good merchantable timber and they know it costs too much to salvage good timber out of a mess of a windfall.
>
> This is not the first time trees have blown down in the woods. Let them rot. Nature will take care of them and the old woods will stay "forever wild" as they should be for the future generations to enjoy.

What did "forever wild" really mean? Harve's answer to the question was delivered in clear and sensible prose. His fear was that dangerous precedents would be set if either the dams were built or the timber salvage was allowed to proceed—precedents that could erode the wilderness quality of the Forest Preserve to the point where it might eventually not be recognizable as wilderness.

As an active member of the Oneida County Forest Preserve Council, Harve had been supportive of that group's efforts to stop the Panther Mountain dam from being built. They had even sued the state for violating the constitution, but on January 9, 1951, Harve took to the opinion pages again, this time in opposition to the Council's position on salvage logging:

> The Oneida County Forest Preserve Council in its action last week unintentionally played into the hands of the loggers who wish to get in on the forest preserve. It is impractical to clean up the scattered windfalls and most certainly could not be done before the next dry spell. The building of roads to the hundreds of windfalls would do great damage, even if it were practical.
>
> As far as the fire hazard is concerned these windfalls catch fire no easier and are no more of a hazard than the visual dry leaves and brush. The proposal by the Forest Preserve Council would tend to commercialize the woods, assisting the old move to lumber the preserve, instead of standing against it.
>
> I think the council made a big mistake.

The interested parties had their answer from Attorney General Goldstein before the end of January. In his opinion, the timber damaged in the big blow-down could be salvaged in order to abate the "menace to the forest preserve," but without an act of the Legislature, there was no authority for the state to "sell or otherwise dispose of the trees."

With swiftness uncommon for business conducted in Albany, the legislature wrote and passed the measures necessary to request bids for the first salvage projects by February 11, 1951. It took eight days. And since the legislation was now free from any further constitutional test, the timber salvage operations continued for the rest of Harve's life and many years longer—44 more years, to be exact. Harve's arguments that there was less danger of forest fires in the windfall than had been had suggested, and that the salvage contracts violated the protection of the constitution, had lost the battle through legal fiat. But another fight was still under way. The fate of the Panther Mountain dam had yet to be decided.

An amendment to the constitution was slated for the ballot in November 1953, which would prevent the construction of river regulating reservoirs like the Panther Mountain project on Forest Preserve land.

When the election was held, the margin of approval of the amendment was almost 2 to 1 in favor, but the legislature apparently didn't get the message. The following year they prepared another amendment that would end up on the ballot in November 1955. That amendment was designed to specifically allow the Panther Mountain dam to be built. The debate smoldered on.

Harve wrote in opposition to the project again, this time quoting an unnamed conservationist who had precisely captured his own sentiment. He sent the letter to the *Utica Daily Press* in March 1955:

> I read your Saturday editorial favoring the Panther Mountain Dam and I disagree with you. Out of all fairness to *Daily Press* readers I hope you will print this section of an editorial which appeared in the *New York Tribune* on March 7.
>
> "The people are sovereign. They can, if they so desire, alter the fine old injunction of the state constitution that the forest preserve shall be 'forever wild.' It is our hope that they will not alter it. Whatever else may be said against the proposed Panther Dam, the fact is that it will be precedent if it is allowed to be built. It will represent a chipping away at one of the precious resources of this state and will portend the day when the New York forest preserve, like so much else of natural grandeur on this continent is subdued and domesticated. The state's heritage should be handed down unspoiled to future citizens."
>
> I thank you.

In the fall of 1955, the wisdom of protecting the forest preserve in the state constitution in 1894 was emphatically validated. The people of New York, for the second time in two years, voted against an amendment that would have allowed the Panther Mountain Dam to be built. It failed by a 3 to 1 margin.

Though the "forever wild" amendment had not stopped the state from salvage logging in the preserve, it did triumph when put to the people concerning the Panther Mountain Dam and the precedent that its construction would have set.

Chapter 23
Adirondack French Louie

IN THE NOVEMBER 20, 1938, EDITION of the *Utica Observer-Dispatch*, E. A. Spears wrote that "Harvey Dunham has collected some 20,000 words about Louie from various persons who knew, saw or heard of him. Someday Dunham will lay before the public the results of his research into the life of the character of the West Canada Lakes."

Fellow *Observer-Dispatch* correspondent David Beetle came to a similar conclusion after interviewing Harve for his book, *West Canada Creek,* in which he wrote, ". . . you could write a book [about French Louie] if you had as many facts as Harvey Dunham."

No one knows exactly when Harve started turning his notes into a book, but after over twenty years of enjoyable labor he did just that. Employing all the skills of his graphic arts training and at his own expense, Harve self-published *Adirondack French Louie: Early Life in the North Woods* in the summer of 1952. It was a two-hundred page history of the Southern Adirondacks wrapped roughly around Louie

Seymour's interesting life. It had been a tedious task, writing, editing, proof-reading, and designing, but now the ink was dry and the binder's glue had set. Harve finally held the first copy in his hands. Now all he had to do was sell them.

To promote the book, Harve sent out dozens of review copies and contracted with Howard Thomas, the owner of Prospect Books and author of numerous regional publications, to help him sell them. For his work, Thomas received ten percent—forty cents for each copy sold. Within weeks the first reviews appeared. They were all encouraging.

The *Waterville Times* wrote, "Harvey L. Dunham has given us a vivid life of 'Louie . . .' We congratulate Mr. Dunham on his most interesting account."

Mortimer Norton, an outdoor writer for many periodicals, wrote, "No person who is interested in Adirondack lore should be without a copy of this book, for it is replete with events, people, and places that have made history in the North Woods."

Harve used a portion of one of the more colorful reviews in a flyer he created to advertise the book (shown on the following page.) In that review, Michael Kernan Jr. of the *Watertown Daily Times* wrote:

> French Louie, the old Adirondack guide, has been rescued from the obscuring mists of legend and hearsay. Mr. Dunham has produced an anecdotal, informal history of the North Woods, for Louie's story is the story of the Adirondacks themselves. The haunting atmosphere of a wild, virgin Adirondacks, which few alive remember, and none, perhaps, will ever see again, is wonderfully captured.

Harve's folksy style had struck a chord with outdoorsmen and women, genealogy buffs and anybody interested in reading about the pioneer days in the Adirondacks. The book was informative without scholarly pretense and as funny and irreverent as Louie and his peers had been during their lives. French Louie's homespun exclamation "Ba da holy feesh" brought smiles to many faces.

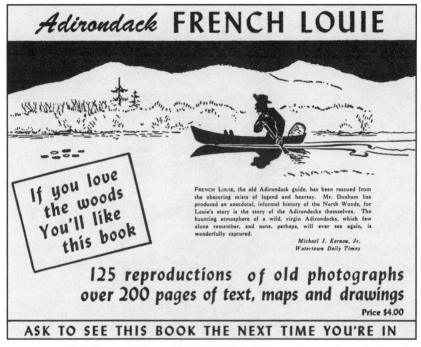

E. A. Spears, who had predicted in 1938 that Harve would someday share "the results of his research," concluded after reading the book that "It is just as well Dunham came along at this time to provide a whiff of those days largely in the past century, for there aren't many people left to tell about them and the backwoods of old and its ways. Louie died in 1915. Therefore the volume may be placed alongside of other Americana." That was high praise coming from Spears, because few men knew more about Louie than he did. He was born in Northwood, NY, a hamlet extinguished underwater when Hinckley Reservoir was filled and who had spent time with Louie at West Lake as a young man in 1906.

With good reviews and positive word-of-mouth advertising, Harve sold out his first run of 2,000 books within a year. In 1953 he made some revisions and ran a second printing, another 2,000 copies, including several more photos and fifteen additional pages.

Some people never find their calling in life. After his book was so warmly received Harve may have breathed a sigh of relief and thought to himself that he had found his.

Chapter 24

A Grave Matter

HARVE'S BOOK INSPIRED MANY READERS to travel to Louie's old haunts. Hunters found his so-called cave with a log bunk and fireplace at the foot of the southeast side of a knob called Cobble Hill, while others flew in to see Louie's fireplace on "Big West" with bush pilots like Bud "Windy" Windhausen, Merrill Phoenix, Clyde Elliott and Norton "Bus" Bird. Backpackers took to long trails from Perkins Clearing, the Moose River Plains or the Cedar River Flow to get there. Once at Louie's Clearing on West Lake they could camp or explore the nearby wilderness as far in as they dared to go.

Although few of them would ever know Louis Seymour personally, many felt like they did know him through Harve's story. Standing in the clearing where Louie's cabin once stood only enhanced that sense. At that place, so removed from civilization, one gets a feeling that few who experience it will ever forget.

Riding his wave of success and perhaps encouraged by the attention he had mustered for himself and Louie, Harve took to the newspapers again in August 1954. This time it was a plea for help about something that had bothered him for years, but had been out of his means or ability to effect. It was about Louie's grave—he had been laid to rest with no marker. Harve hoped others might now agree with him that Louie deserved a memorial, so he wrote to rally financial support to purchase a proper gravestone. The no-nonsense headline in the *Utica Observer-Dispatch* read: "Grave Matter."

Utican Seeks Marker for French Louie

"It's about time French Louie lying up there in the cemetery in an unmarked grave at Speculator had a headstone," said Harvey L. Dunham, 5 Irving Place, as he started today a one-man drive to buy the stone, price about $60.

French Louie was an interesting character who lived for decades mostly alone in his line of woodland camps from Moose River to Pillsbury Lake, but chiefly at his headquarters at the source of the West Canada Creek—the West Canada Lakes.

Louis Seymour, better known as "French Louie" died February 28, 1915 of pneumonia in Speculator and on the afternoon of the funeral the school was closed for the funeral and the children carried sprays of evergreen in honor of the Frenchman. That was nearly forty years ago and said Dunham. Johnny Leaf, the Indian trapper, has a headstone in Wilmurt. French Louie should have one in Speculator

Harve's appeal strummed the heartstrings of fans and pledges rolled in for the cause. In September, a second report announced the results of Harve's campaign. From the *Utica Observer-Dispatch,* September 17, 1954:

Louie Will Get Belated Marker

Louie Seymour, lone man of the West Canada Lakes, famed for woodcraft and made more famous by a book Harvey L. Dunham of Utica wrote about him, is going to have a headstone.

Dunham said today that $63 has been contributed for a headstone for "French Louie," who died at Speculator in 1915. Louis was about 85 at his death.

The author of *Adirondack French Louie* had an idea a few weeks ago that it was time a headstone was set on the grave. Contributions rolled in.

An Amsterdam man wrote: "Wait, I'm going to collect some money from others who knew about Louie." He sent $17.

A woman whose father knew Louie contributed $10 "in Memory."

Carmine V. Amaroia, proprietor of the Virtu Memorial Company, Oneida and Prospect St., Utica, will provide the headstone.

When told it was for "French Louie," he displayed a lively interest and said:

"I've read about French Louie in the *Observer-Dispatch* and I'll give you a special price."

Up in Speculator, John L. Aird will build a base for the stone. It will be in place early in October. . . . Now Louie will have a headstone.

It wasn't a lot of money, but it was more than Harve had and he was buoyed by the response. The smallest offerings—dimes, quarters and dollars—seemed to mean the most,

but all recognized the importance of remembering, lest the remaining inhabitants forget the toils of their predecessors.

Harve's book was as much a history of a region as it was of one man. So too, Louie was becoming a symbol for the lifestyle of an era that had passed.

Regardless of what it meant to the contributors, Louie had a memorial at last.

Chapter 25
A Grandfatherly Influence

Donna Pierce

ONNA PIERCE JONES WAS ABOUT TEN YEARS OLD when she first met Harvey Dunham, "in either 1952 or '53." She remembers him as "a gentleman, a prankster," a grandfatherly figure and "a mentor." Her paternal grandfather, Harry Pierce, knew Harvey from hunting and fishing trips and had recommended to Donna's parents, Dan and Dawn Pierce of Binghamton, N.Y., that they rent Fraser Clearing to see if they liked the area. The Pierce family was already familiar with the surroundings at West Canada Creek, having tent-camped there in the past. Donna's parents had even honeymooned there, as Bob Gillespie's daughter Helen and her husband had done.[17]

[17] The story of Ruth Gillespie's honeymoon appears on page 165.

The Pierce family story goes that during the honeymoon the newly wedded couple got caught in a downpour and sought refuge under the cover of Trume Haskell's camp porch. As the bride and groom began to dry out, Dawn watched in dismay as her wedding gown began to dry and shrink. When the dress finished shrinking, it was nearly the length of the yet-to-be-invented mini-skirt, exposing her silk slip, which had retained its former length and flowed down below her knees.

The rental of the camp at Fraser Clearing was a successful adventure for the whole family, daughters Donna, Gail and Kathryn ("Kay") and their dog Inkiferd Spot, who they usually called just Spot. The family enjoyed the camp so thoroughly that they began driving from Binghamton nearly every weekend. The lure of the Adirondacks was a pleasant contrast to their Southern Tier region and it wasn't long before they rented it for the rest of the season and then booked it for the entire following year. Needless to say, the charm and hospitality of their landlord greatly contributed to their "West Crick" experience.

Above: Dan Pierce.
Left: (left to right, back row) Frank Willey, Harve Dunham, Kay Pierce on her mother Dawn's lap. On the ground, Donna and Gail Pierce and Inkiferd Spot, their dog.

The Pierces became nearly a second family to Dunham. Harve's daughter, Jean, had married Beardslie Keck of Montvale, N.J., and they had a son, David, but they were less interested in "roughing it" in woods than the Pierces, so the Pierces provided a family style of friendship to Harve that he really enjoyed. As Donna put it, "There was nothing pretentious about us. We were just good old folks and we were company for him."

Donna, the oldest of the three Pierce girls, had many fond recollections of life at Fraser Clearing and the influence that Harve Dunham had in her life. First, she described the trip from Binghamton to camp:

From the first of March through the end of October, every Friday night we would be in the car, packed and ready to go when Dad got off from work and we'd be on the way. We'd go right up Route 12, right through Utica and right up to Camp. We'd get there at nine, ten o'clock at night and have to walk in with flashlights. At Nobleboro on Route 8 there was a hot dog stand at the corner of Haskell Road. That's where you turned. A sawmill and lumberyard was next on the right. A little farther down was the old Haskell Place—which used to be Wilkinson's—and beyond that is a place everybody knows as "flat rock," where the road runs right across the top of a big flat rock. From there you could cross the West Canada on an old bridge that went to a logging camp on the other side, or, as we did, you

Beneath the bridge at Flat Rock was a popular spot for the Pierces to picnic.

continued straight and at that point, the road stopped. There was a little creek with a bridge across it that the State would take down to stop cars from passing. There was a gatekeeper's house there too.

That was where everyone parked their Doodle Bugs, in Green's Clearing. Doodle Bugs were the stripped-down old cars that people used to get into the

A gaggle of Doodle Bugs at Green's Clearing.

woods and there were probably seventy of them there. Now, you didn't leave your battery in the car, because if you did, someone would steal it. The batteries were always going flat or dying, so people would take parts off each others' cars in order to get their car up in the woods. Sometimes you got them back and sometimes you didn't. Harvey's car was "Harvey's Headache." It was green and he had painted "Harvey's Headache" on the side of it.

Up from there was a larger bridge, which is still there, over Big Brook; then you go about a mile and a half up. At the bottom of the second hill there's a driveway and that's where Fraser Clearing is. Peachy's place was just before that. On the hill above the Fraser Clearing Camp is Eagle's Nest, and the Seabury Dam is down below on the West Canada.

That was how the trip on the old Chevarie Tote Road to Fraser Clearing went. In the summertime you would hear the hoot owls—an amazing sound—and if Harvey knew that we were coming, and if he could get the car running, he sometimes waited for us at the gate and took us up in the Doodle Bug. That was a wonderful treat, because when you're fourteen years old you don't always want to walk two miles in the dark with everything needed for camp loaded into pack baskets to carry. My mother had a tendency to make those pack baskets pretty darn heavy.

Harve and a friend work both ends of a cross-cut saw. Harve's Doodle Bug behind them sports the car's name, "Harvey's Headache."

After they were at camp for a while, if a Doodle Bug was coming they would hear it from nearly a mile away. Donna described what happened next. "When we stayed at camp all summer it could get lonely there, so we kids would run up to the road to see who was going by and wave. Whenever Harvey came he would wave and shout 'Segoolie,' and that was how he welcomed us."

Once they were settled in, Harve showed the Pierces all the wonderful sites that he had indicated on his illustrated flyers years before. He took them to Wild Cat Cliff and High Falls on the Baby Lake outlet. "We went over a stone bridge," Donna recalled, "hiked sixteen miles to Nat Shepard's Camp and back, right in the middle of nowhere, with three little kids and a Cocker Spaniel. Harvey, I think, just got a big kick out of the little girls up there being tomboys. I was as much a Tom Sawyer as any Tom Sawyer or Huck Finn ever was."

The Pierces visit Millers Camp II. Back row, Kay Pierce with Don Smith. John Dye is in front of them. Front row, left to right, Dan Pierce (standing), "Judge" Wiliby, Donna & Dawn Pierce and Jim Parker. The others could not be identified.

A tomboy spirit was certainly helpful the day they explored around the Klock Flow and Miller's Camp, seven miles north of Fraser Clearing. Donna took a tumble of ten or fifteen feet that day and remembered looking up as they all stood around wondering if she was going to get up. But she shook herself back to consciousness. "That would have been a long way to go for help if I had broken something," she said. "But we were tough. We had to be. I walked all the way back."

They visited Trume Haskell at his camp and were introduced to his pets. Behind the cabin Trume had a cold-spring fed pool where swam captive brook trout. He also had pet snakes, including one named Ralph. "You respected the snakes," said Donna, "because they took care of the insects in Trume's garden." That was a trick he had learned from old French Louie.

When given the chance, Harve showed off his prankster side to the children. "He was a bit of a ventriloquist," Donna recalled. "Peachy

Barse the hermit had died, but Harvey convinced us kids that he was alive and well and living in his camp, and Harve would go in the camp and he'd shake the bunk and say, 'Come on Peachy get up. Get up. The girls are here, it's time to play.' And then he'd throw his voice and say 'Go away. Don't bother me, I'm sleeping. I had a rough night last night.'" Other times, he'd have them convinced that he was talking to someone in the woods when there was no one there at all.

To help them pass the time, Harve instigated innumerable activities for the Pierce girls. He taught them to paddle a canoe properly and how to build a raft with pulp logs that had hung up on the shore years before during the river drives. He inspired artistic projects too, such as collecting shelf fungi or "conks" and showing them how to engrave pictures with captions on them using a straightened paper clip or a jackknife.

One time he and Donna each whittled bare a piece of kindling wood and then inscribed this bit of woodsman's wisdom on them, "He who cuts his own wood is warm twice." They hung the carvings up on the wall over the stoves in each of the camps.

Donna and Gail Pierce get a lesson in raft building and sailing from Harve.

He encouraged the girls to draw—anything and everything—and taught them to notice their natural surroundings.

Harve taught the family what he knew about some of the native plant species and their traditional uses. He identified many trees, the spruce for its gum; bracken ferns for fiddleheads, and bee balm for Oswego tea. He showed them how to eat elderberry blossoms, and had a trick in mind when he instructed them on "Jack in the Pulpit." He cut a piece of the root for each one in the family and then had them eat it. "Gag," Donna said, "very bitter! He made sure to give Dad the biggest dose though! It has a paralyzing effect," Harve told them afterwards. "The Indians used it if they had to pull teeth."

Harve read poems to the girls, his own and those of others. He encouraged Donna to find the poetry of Robert Frost in the library, and she did.

Then there was writing. Adding to the camp log book was a mandatory writing activity. Donna recounted, "One of the things I would do every Sunday at Harvey's request was to write in the log book. It was very, very important to him that the log be kept on a weekly basis. You just did it. It was expected. I was the eldest, so it was my job. While everybody else was breaking camp, I was to note the weather, the conditions, what the fishing was like, what we did, anybody who visited, if a hoot-owl was heard during the night, a chronological accounting of our time at camp."

Back home during the winter, the Pierces began exchanging letters with Harve. Donna even sent Harve a copy of her book report one year and he critiqued it and mailed it back. It certainly helped that the book report was about *Adirondack French Louie*.

Around Christmas time each year, the family waited in expectation for one of Harve's custom-made Christmas cards. He created a new design every year.

Best of all, Donna said, "Harve taught us that it was okay to be silly, even as an adult; that it was okay to have fun."

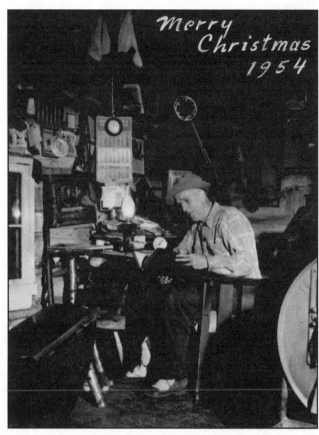

*Harve's 1954
Christmas card
to the Pierces.*

Though she knew Harve for only four or five years—and though she may not have known it was happening at the time—the adventures and activities that Donna experienced via Harve's teaching and example profoundly influenced the rest of her life. She referred to some specific examples of events that opened her eyes to a career path that she says she wouldn't have known about or considered had she not met Harvey Dunham.

She recalled a day that Harve brought her to his workplace at Mohawk Engraving in Utica, to give her a taste of his illustrator's trade. "I sat on a stool and watched him do paste-ups and mechanicals, the old way, before computers," she said. But what Harve showed her next seemed "almost like magic."

There is a horse drawing a lumber wagon and the wagon had metal wheels with rubber tires and he didn't think that was appropriate for his book, so with an air-brush, he took out the rubber tires and put wooden-spoked, metal-rimmed wheels. If you look closely now you can see where it's been doctored. I think the book had already come out, so I don't know if he was doing it for a second edition or whether he was just demonstrating to me what it was to use an air brush, but I can remember sitting there watching him do this and being in total awe.

Interestingly, the picture that Donna described is not in the first (1952) printing of the book, but is in the second (1953) edition. A picture captioned "Scoot 'N Drag" is within a group of photographs that appear before page 130. Looking closely at the picture, you can see the wooden wheels have been drawn in, making it likely that Donna was witness to the creation of the artwork that actually appeared in the 1953 edition.

Thirty years later Donna was teaching college students the handicraft that Harve had demonstrated. Of her students she said, "I taught them how to use boards, T-squares, rubber cement and wax; illustrating and copy writing and editing; I taught them graphic design."

My bachelor's degree is in fine arts, my first master's degree is in art education and my second one is from Syracuse University in advertising design. There's no one in my family who did anything like that at all, so when you stop to analyze, how did I get involved, who sparked the interest, how did I get on that road as a sixteen-year-old when a guidance counselor asked me "what do you want to do in your life?" Of course, this was 1964, so if you were a college-bound girl, where did they send you? You're going to be a teacher or a nurse and I didn't want to be a nurse. "So what discipline do you want to teach?" I'm going to be an art teacher.

So when I say that Harvey was my mentor, I think that he's the one who realized there was a creative person who needed some guidance and I think he was the one who said "go for it kid. You can be an illustrator, you can be a designer, this is what illustrators do, this is what designers do, this is what writers do," and he made it fun. Look at *French Louie;* look at the things he wrote. Grammar was not always necessary; spelling was not always necessary; he didn't get all out of shape if you misspelled something.

He was promoting the creative when everyone else was promoting the structured and at a time in life when I needed someone to say it's okay to write silly stories or it's all right to write funny poems or you can just wing it!

"I'm telling you all this," she said, "to give you a feeling for the man that I knew."

By Christmas time 1955, Harve was ill with cancer, though he never spoke of it, at least not to the children. Shortly after Christmas, Harve sent a letter and addressed it "Dear all, but not Spot." Apparently Spot had absconded with a "Segoolie Special Hamburger" without asking permission that summer, and the unkind act was never forgotten. Harve wrote:

> I didn't undo your package when it came. I put it under the tree. Nothing I had gave me the pleasure of receiving like that. Even if you kids had found a common little Hemlock cone and wrapped it up in a note, "Merry Christmas" with your name, it still would have given me more pleasure to receive than anything else. But with all that work that you put on them and the way that they were done up and the letters it made a very merry Christmas.
>
> So you're going to Fraser Clearing over New Year's. For a good many years we always spent New Year's at camp, many times before the lumbering, going in on snowshoes and more than once walking from Nobleboro. Those were tough trips, but we could take it.
>
> Tell Dan I always put chains on at Nobleboro. I never owned snow tires.

A Doodle Bug on the tote road in winter.

I was up the week before Christmas—almost a foot and a half of snow. The gate is open and the road is perfect. Keep note of passing places so if a load of logs looms up ahead of you, you know where you've got to back up to on the road.

I don't remember if I threw the key across the creek or whether I took it back in the woods and buried it. Anyway here is another key that you can keep and put on your key ring. The key holder you gave me, Donna, I was examining it. It looks like you laced that around the edge yourself. Darn good. Gail's panorama and Kay's art too.

Dan, go up to the little shed back of the little log cabin and get some of those old dry split slabs. I know there's some left there. They will give you a hot quick fire to get some birch going. And if Bill left any coal, be sure to use it, especially for a night fire.

There must be ten inches of ice on the Stillwater. You could take a hike on it from Kay Lake to Segoolie, but from Kay Lake to the dam is always treacherous, I suppose on account of the current.

I know you had a Merry Christmas. Imagine Donna, Gail and Kay at Christmas time. Wonderful for you Dawn, three kids like that.

Now I'll sign off, wishing you a very Happy New Year. You ought to write it up for that log at Fraser Clearing.

Harve

Below: Harve Dunham standing behind his camp at Fraser Clearing. Right: The view from where he was standing, looking upstream from the foot of the Seabury Stillwater.

"The last time I saw Harvey in the woods," Donna recalled, "was New Year's Day, 1956. We were staying at the camp and he came in and he was wearing a white shirt, bright red suspenders and a beaver skin top hat. He had walked on snowshoes from Segoolie to Fraser Clearing to spend New Year's with us. And then he got back on his snowshoes and walked away."

That was exactly how Harve wanted them to remember him.

Chapter 26
The End of the Trail

Beyond the Last Old Blaze

Some day, perhaps, I shall have time to go,
Farther in,
Beyond the last old blaze,
Where there are no trails
But paths, where deer come down to drink,
That lead nowhere.
And when I unsling my pack on that far lake
I'll sit awhile and think
Of all the dreams I've had about that very place.
Who laughs at dreams?
They do not know the trips I've had
Before the open fire on winter nights
When with topographic maps I hit the trail.
Little Rock, I see it now,
Deep set between close curving contour lines
Made to remind one of blue reflected skies
And mountains steep and dark with noble pines.
And yet, some day, perhaps, I'll just pack up and go.

—Harvey L. Dunham, 1926

HARVE'S GOOD FRIEND Lloyd Blankman wrote that Harve "loved the woods more than any man I ever knew and he could write about it." Author Paul F. Jamieson described Harvey this way: "Dunham was a woodsman by hobby, a commercial artist in Utica by vocation, and a literary artist by accident."

Left to right: Harvey Dunham, Billy Collyer and Lloyd Blankman strumming and singing on a winter afternoon.

Harve's research became part of his life. In a way, the book *Adirondack French Louie* came to define Harve's life; it was his defining accomplishment. He may have had other stories to tell, but we will never know. Cancer took him away before any further projects began. He died on July 24, 1956, in his sixty-ninth year, less than four years after his book's publication.

He had only a short time to enjoy its success, but he'd probably be pleased to know that it's still in print today. "Many thousands of copies" have been sold, according to the book's current publisher, Rob Igoe, President of North Country Books, Inc.

Sharing French Louie's legacy with generations of new readers who appreciated the Adirondacks and their history was clearly one of Harve's goals. At the end of the book he wrote:

> The hunting grounds are no longer free and no longer can anyone kill game at will and build his cabin wherever his fancy dictates. Louie and his generation are gone and no one will ever take their place.

A drawing of French Louie by Frank Devecis that wasn't used in the book.

"An affectionate dear old fellow." "A wonderful character with the best of principles, who always minded his own business." "Harmless as a kitten." "Independent old cuss." "As honest as the sunshine." So Louie is remembered by those who knew him.

His name will be legend. Those who were not so fortunate to have known Louie in the flesh will know him in the spirit. His name will be spoken for years to come around the evening campfires.

Harve's old friend Bob Gillespie would have been proud of his partner's perseverance and publishing success. His encouragement to "keep writing" twenty years earlier certainly hadn't gone unheeded.

The newspapers that announced the passing of Louie's biographer ran the gamut from the tiniest North Country newspapers all the way up to the "Old Grey Lady," The *New York Times*. Utica's own *Observer-Dispatch* carried this copy.

July 25, 1956

Harvey Dunham Dies at 69; Author of 'French Louie'

Funeral Services for Harvey L. Dunham, 69, of 5 Irving Place will be held, at 2 p.m. Friday from the Gordon Funeral Home, 6 Steuben Park, with the Rev. Paul A. Roy, pastor of Central Methodist Church, officiating. Mr. Dunham, author of *Adirondack French Louie*, biography of the famed Adirondack hermit and trapper, Louis Seymour,

died July 24, 1956 in Faxton Hospital after a brief illness. Interment will be in New Forest Cemetery.

Mr. Dunham was born in Sauquoit, Oct. 6, 1891, a son of Flora Jones Dunham and the late Frank Dunham. He was educated in Utica Schools and attended art school in Philadelphia and New York.

Mr. Dunham was a commercial artist and worked in New York, Albany, Washington and Baltimore. For several years he had worked in Utica at Mohawk Engraving Company. He was married Aug. 12, 1912 to Bessie Throop. She died in Albany in 1914.

He attended Central Methodist Church and served in the Merchant Marine in World War I. He was a member of the Ancient Lodge F & a.m. and the Knights Templar in Albany. Surviving are his mother, a daughter, Mrs. Beardslie Keck, Montvale, NJ, a sister Miss Florence L. Dunham, Utica, a grandson, David Keck, Montvale, NJ and two nieces.

Harve and friends enjoy a relaxing evening inside Segoolie, 1952.

It seems fitting here to repeat the last lines penned by Harve on the closing page of *Adirondack French Louie.*

And now the old man knocks the ashes out of his pipe on the toe of his boot.

He has told his story, the story of Louie and the West Creek.

The night is peaceful. The punkies aren't biting. The low roar of the creek as it pours through the rotting sluiceways of the old lumber dam does not really break the stillness. The tall black spruce and balsam are silhouetted against the moonlit mist of the stillwater. The opposite shoreline and the woods are veiled in soft mystic light and the moon rides high over the mountains. It is late and time to go.

"Good night, oldtimer!"

"Well, so long."

"So long."

Harvey Dunham reading by candle light.
The heading on the page reads "The Open Road."

Epilogue
A Lasting Impact

I T'S INTERESTING NOW, to look back to the beginning of this
project about these fine men and the places they travelled. We
knew so little about them when we started. Now they feel like
old friends.

Bob Gillespie, of course, died too young, or so it seems from this
side of the grass. But his guiding influence, sense of humor and love of
the woods inspired his daughters, grandchildren and his friends.

Now his story and photographs can be shared with future generations, to hopefully inspire his same sense of adventure and curiosity
and the joy of a good tramp in the woods.

There is no doubt that Bob had a big influence on Harve and Ray Dunham too. Had either of them given a eulogy for Bob, either in church or in a quiet aside with some common friends, it would have been interesting to hear what they would have had to say. It's hard to believe that Bob was ever too far from Harve's thoughts. His hand was in all aspects of the West Canada Creek camps. He helped drive the nails and fix the roofs and carry the stoves. Bob's picture hung on the wall at Segoolie until the day Harve died. Harve kept all of Bob's letters too.

Bob's passing may have helped Harve to realize that he had something important to accomplish and that no one else would keep him on that task. That sense of making the most of the time he had might have helped him to finish his book after all those years of collecting stories.

When we started, as interested as we were in Louie Seymour and his biography, we didn't expect more from Harve. Louie was enough, and simply finding the foundation of some of Harve's inspiration would have been plenty, but each new fact, every article we found that Harve had written seemed to lead us somewhere else. In the end some had to be left out, so here are a few stories that we followed after Harve passed away, to see what transpired.

At West Lake

In November 1938, the Conservation Commission wrote to Harve, promising that they would leave the old fireplace alone as a memento to Louie. They kept their word. A new Ranger Station was eventually built in 1950, adjacent to the fireplace, where it stood for thirty-seven years when it became the subject of its own controversy. At some point during the 1980s the cabin was slated for removal because of a new and stricter interpretation of the term "wilderness" during the development of the Adirondack Park State Land Master Plan. The plan deemed that the cabin was a "non-conforming use" and was slated to be removed.

The local rangers, many of whom had visited or lived at the remote station, were so strongly opposed to the demolition that they were not asked to assist in the destruction, and in January 1987, with very little commotion, several Department of Environmental Conservation (DEC) employees flew in to West Lake with a helicopter and burned the cabin to the ground. Louie's fireplace, however, was again left unscathed. Here's why. French Louie's fireplace had been added to the list of historic sites in the "Adirondack Park State Land Master Plan." Nearly fifty years after Harve began his original appeal, long after he would ever know it had happened, the state recognized the importance of (and lack of harm in) keeping the fireplace as a wilderness monument to French Louie Seymour—and to Harvey Dunham's work to see that it was protected.

Salvage Logging Ends—After Forty-Four Years

In 1950 and '51, Harve opined against salvage logging after the 1950 "big blow-down," arguing that 1) there was nothing to worry about, trees fall all the time, 2) there was little greater chance that a windfall would start a fire than would the normal leaves and tinder, 3) the act of getting in and out of the woods and building roads would "do many times more damage than the value of what little timber they could salvage," and 4) "lumbermen have to be very choosy in cutting good merchantable timber and they know it costs too much to salvage good timber out of a mess of a windfall."

Regardless of arguments like his, salvage cutting as an "emergency measure" was approved by the Attorney General, passed through the Legislature and signed by the Governor in a process that circumvented the "forever wild" amendment to the constitution, making it virtually impossible to stop.

Subsequently, salvage lumbering continued for forty-four years until another big blow-down occurred in 1995 and the DEC decided to reassess. DEC hired an advisory committee of consulting ecologists and assembled a report based on the scientists' recommendations and its own internal assessment of the consequences of storm damage and salvage logging. They concluded that salvage logging on protected lands could no longer be ecologically or economically justified, essentially the same conclusion that Harve had come to forty-five years earlier.

Governor Pataki accepted the recommendation, and a "no-salvage" decision was adopted. "Forever wild" was once again the over-riding law of the preserve.

The Seabury Stillwater. Segoolie at its head, Fraser Clearing at its foot.

The West Canada Creek Camps

When Harve died he left the Segoolie Camp to his daughter Jean Dunham Keck and her husband Beardslie Keck, and the camps at Fraser Clearing to the Pierce family. This fact lends weight to Donna Pierce Jones' account of Harve and his influence on her life. The Kecks sold Segoolie long ago to friends of the Pierces. The Pierces still own and treasure Fraser Clearing.

Adirondack French Louie

Of course the biggest and most lasting impact that Harve made—and is still making—is through his fantastic book *Adirondack French Louie—Early Life in the North Woods*. If you haven't read it you should. If you haven't read it in a few years, it might be time to read it again.

Postscript

THE BEST ADVENTURES, large or small, are exciting not only to our physical selves, but to our imaginative sides as well: physical, psychological and spiritual affairs. That is perhaps why such events can often be recalled in such vivid detail. From that point of view, the early 20th century experiences of Bob Gillespie and Harvey Dunham can be more fully appreciated. They braved the wilderness without the conveniences of modern equipment to fish, hunt and explore while taking in stride whatever nature presented them along the way. They experienced absolute and sustained isolation, which allowed them to take stock of themselves, their abilities, their lives, and their connection with the community of woodsmen they held dear. They also took time to reflect and write about their impressions, which enhanced their recollections.

Adirondack Adventures was written so that readers could get to know more about these interesting men and the places they travelled, and to share their experience as much as can be done by reading. But we also want to share this encouragement—the wilderness experience that Gillespie and Dunham enjoyed can still be had today! The protected Adirondacks are ours to enjoy. We hope that their adventures will inspire you to set out on your own adventures. One day maybe your journals will be the ones that others are reading.

For more about French Louie or this book
visit www.frenchlouie.com and www.theforagerpress.com

Not everything we wrote and collected made it into the book, so we'll be adding some of that additional material to our web sites. Pictures and anecdotes will be part of the mix, as well as some "behind the scenes" stories.

If you are related to any of the people in any of our books, or you have information, stories or photographs that might help us improve or correct them, by all means please let us know. You can reach us though our websites, by regular mail or email to info@theforagerpress.com.

And thanks for reading!

Other Books from The Forager Press, LLC:
Life in a North Woods Lumber Camp
By William J. O'Hern, 2012

Noah John Rondeau's Adirondack Wilderness Days:
A Year with the Hermit of Cold River Flow
By William J. O'Hern, 2009

Under An Adirondack Influence:
The Life of A. L. Byron-Curtiss, 1871—1959
By William J. O'Hern and Roy E. Reehil, 2008

Adirondack Characters and Campfire Yarns:
Early Settlers and Their Traditions
By William J. O'Hern, 2005

Coming soon by William J. O'Hern:
Adirondack Kaleidoscope and North Country Characters
Adirondack Memories and Campfire Stories
Adirondack Wilds: Exploring the Haunts of Noah John Rondeau,
Hermit of Cold River

Acknowledgments

OREMOST IN OUR ACKNOWLDGEMENT of the people who contributed to this project are Carolyn Browne Malkin and her brother, Robert C. Browne, whom William O'Hern and I regretfully thank posthumously. Had it not been for their willingness to share their grandfather's wonderful journals and correspondence with Harvey Dunham, this book could never have been written. We also thank Carolyn for opening her home to us, and for graciously sharing anecdotes and stories about her family, many of which we included in the book.

Special thanks also go to George Cataldo, who thought it was a good idea for us to meet his friend Carolyn. It really *was* a good idea, George!

In the process of researching and writing, I had the chance to meet several people whose input became integral to the work. My interview with Donna Pierce Jones was a pleasure to conduct and provided important first-person insight into the life and character of Harvey Dunham. Donna also shared fantastic photographs and maps that helped us to tell this story.

When is an accident considered destiny? My answer lies in my chance meeting with Richard and Kathleen White, a meeting that led to them remembering that they had stored a box that contained most of the artwork and pictures that hung on the walls of Camp Segoolie until it was burned down 1985. That box was a treasure chest. We can't thank you enough for allowing us to use them for the book.

My wife, Patricia Cerro-Reehil, not only put up with my working on this for eight years, but she helped proofread too. Thanks Pat!

Thanks to retired Forest Ranger Captain Paul Hartmann for providing a photograph of the old ranger station at West Lake, from the collection of W. G. Howard, Superintendent of Forests, New York Conservation Department, from 1927 to 1948. The rangers recently received Mr. Howard's collection for preservation.

Thanks also to Eric Kessler, Trume Haskell's grandson, for inviting me to take a tour of the old camp, visit with his friends and inspect the camp log books for any entries denoting meetings between Harvey Dunham and his grandfather. This one was most interesting:

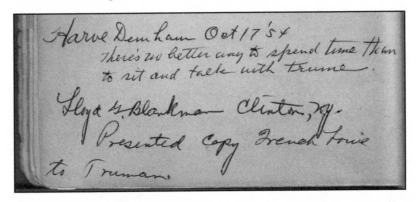

I'm not sure how many times I visited the Adirondack Museum Library over the eight years that we have been working on this project, but I do know that Jerold Pepper, the director of the library, was incredibly accommodating each time we visited and Angela Donnelly, the manager of historic photographs and films, was as well. Thank you both for your patience and assistance.

Neal Burdick did an excellent job—as he always does—as our lead editor, scholarly advisor and for this book, the author of our introduction. Mary L. Thomas also helped out with editing. Thank you both very much.

For help in proofreading and manuscript review, we gratefully acknowledge Edward Blankman, Barbara Reehil, Gary Lee, Julie Simpson, Donna Pierce Jones and Richard and Kathleen White. Mr. Blankman also allowed us to use several photographs from his father Lloyd Blankman's personal collection.

In closing I'd like to thank my coauthor, William "Jay" O'Hern, for recognizing my passion for everything "West Canada" and for allowing me to run with my vision of this project. It is a pleasure to work with you.

—*Roy E. Reehil*

Bibliography

BOOKS

Beetle, David H. *West Canada Creek*. Utica, NY: Utica Observer-Dispatch, 1946.

De Sormo, Maitland C. *The Heydays of the Adirondacks*. Saranac Lake, NY: Adirondack Yesteryears, Inc., 1974.

Donaldson, Alfred Lee. *A History of the Adirondacks*. New York, NY: The Century Company, 1921. 2v.

Dunham, Harvey Leslie. *Adirondack French Louie: Early Life in the North Woods*. Utica, NY: Self Published, 1952.

———. *Adirondack French Louie: Early Life in the North Woods*. 2nd Edition. Utica, NY: Self Published, 1953.

Harter, Henry A. *Fairy Tale Railroad: The Mohawk and Malone from the Mohawk, through the Adirondacks to the St. Lawrence*. Utica, NY: North Country Books, Inc., 1979.

Longstreth, T. Morris. *The Adirondacks*. New York, NY: The Century Company, 1917.

Marleau, William R. *Big Moose Station*. Inlet, NY: Marleau Family Press, 1986.

McMartin, Barbara. *The Great Forest of the Adirondacks*. Utica, NY: North Country Books, Inc., 1994.

O'Hern, William J. *Adirondack Characters and Campfire Yarns: Early Settlers and their Traditions*. Cleveland, NY: The Forager Press, LLC, 2005.

Schaefer, Paul. *Adirondack Explorations: Nature Writings of Verplanck Colvin*. Syracuse, NY: Syracuse University Press, 1997.

Schneider, Paul. *The Adirondacks*. New York, NY: Henry Holt and Company, LLC, 1997.

The Big Moose Lake History Project. *Big Moose Lake: In the Adirondacks*. Syracuse, NY: The Big Moose Lake History Project, 2004.

Wallace, Edwin. *Descriptive Guide to the Adirondacks*. Syracuse, NY: Watson Gill, 1889.

MAGAZINES

Dunham, Harvey L. "French Louie." *New York Folklore Quarterly*, August, 1946, Vol. 2.

Kenwell, Gerald. "French Lewie." *New York State Conservationist*, August–September, 1952.

NEWSPAPERS

Dunham, Harvey L., "Keep French Lewey's Fireplace." *Utica Observer-Dispatch*, September 23, 1938.

———. "Opinion." *Utica Daily Press*, October, 1949.

———. "Opinion." *Utica Daily Press*, October, 1950.

———. "Opinion." *Utica Daily Press*, January, 1951.

———. "Opinion." *Utica Daily Press*, November 9, 1951.

———. "Opinion." *Utica Daily Press*, March, 1955.

Spears, E. A., "In the lore of the North Country, French Lewey Was a Pioneer of the Adirondacks." *Utica Observer-Dispatch,* Novemebr 20, 1938.

———. "Utican's New Book Recalls Early Days Along West Canada." *Utica Observer-Dispatch,* June 22, 1952.

Unsigned, "A. Vanderbilt Wedding." *New York Times,* December 21, 1881.

———. "Hope for the Forests." *New York Times,* May 9, 1885.

———. "New Forestry Bill." *New York Times,* May 11, 1885.

———. "The Passing Away of the Forests." *New York Times,* August 1, 1889.

———. "The People's Park in the Adirondacks." *New York Times,* August 21, 1889.

———. "For an Adirondack Park." *New York Times,* April 23, 1890.

———. "For a State Forest Park." *New York Times,* May 24, 1890.

———. "May in the Adirondacks." *New York Times,* May 25, 1890.

———. "Plans for a Forest Park." *New York Times,* October 23, 1890.

———. "For an Adirondack Preserve." *New York Times,* January 23, 1891.

———. "The Adirondack Forest Park." *New York Times,* April 26, 1891.

———. "W. Seward Webb's Road." *New York Times,* May 14, 1891.

———. "Save the Adirondacks." *New York Times,* May 15, 1891.

———. "The The Forestry Preserve." *New York Times,* May 16, 1891.

———. "The Adirondack Railroad." *New York Times,* May 18, 1891.

———. "Paid Big Lawyers Fees." *New York Times,* May 22, 1891.

———. "The Adirondacks Threatened." *New York Times,* May 27, 1891.

———. "Keep Out of the Forests." *New York Times,* May 28, 1891.

———. "The Law is Plain Enough." *New York Times,* May 31, 1891.

———. "The Big Forest In Danger." *New York Times,* June 10, 1891.

———. "Dr. Webb's Plans." *New York Times,* June 20, 1891.

———. "By Permission of Dr. Webb." *New York Times,* June 29, 1891.

———. "Dr. Webb's Plan Modified." *New York Times,* July 16, 1891.

———. "Sport in the Adirondacks." *New York Times,* August 10, 1891.

———. "Dr. Webb's Railroad." *New York Times,* August 27, 1891.

———. "To Build on State Land," *New York Times,* September 11, 1891.

———. "Dr. Webb's New Railroad," *New York Times,* Novemebr 20, 1891.

———. "Beaver River Dam." *Watertown Times,* December 1, 1982.

———. "Webb's Adirondack Road." *New York Times,* January 14, 1892.

———. "Adirondack Park Bill." *New York Times,* May 21, 1892.

———. "Bought by the Central." *New York Times,* August 9, 1892.

———. "Venerable Elmira Free Academy Graduates Another Class." *Elmira Daily Gazette and Free Press,* June 21, 1894.

———. "Tour of the Adirondacks." *Oswego Daily Palladium,* July 26, 1894.

———. "An Adirondack Club." *New York Times,* July 7, 1894.

———. "To Preserve the Forest Lands." *New York Times,* August 24, 1894.

———. "Under the New Constitution." *New York Times,* November 12, 1894.

———. "Dr. Webb's Flooded Land." *New York Times,* January 11, 1895.

———. "Dr. W. Seward Webb's Claim." *New York Times,* January 12, 1895.

———. "To Protect the Forests." *New York Times,* January 28, 1895.

———. "Dr. Webb's Damaged Property." *New York Times,* July 23, 1895.

———. "For Violation of Game Laws." *Gloversville Daily Leader,* September 10, 1895.

———. "Will Buy Webb's Land." *New York Times,* December 7, 1895.

———. "The Adirondacks Amendment." *New York Times,* October 28, 1896.

———. "Untitled Announcements." *Utica Sunday Journal,* July 14, 1901.

———. "State Lands for Private Parks." *Brooklyn Daily Eagle,* October 22, 1905.

———. "Still Sets His Traps." *Albany Evening Journal,* February 1, 1909.

———. "Funeral of Bessie Throop Dunham held This Afternoon." *Utica Herald-Dispatch,* June 16, 1914.

———. "Bessie May Throop Dunham Obituary." *Waterville Times,* June 16, 1914.

———. "Come Out of Adirondacks for First Time in Lives to See the Sights of City." *Syracuse Post-Standard,* February 25, 1915.

———. "Adirondack Guide is Lost Where Trees Have no Moss." *Syracuse Post-Standard,* February 26, 1915.

———. "Guide and Family Glad to Return to the Woods." *Syracuse Post-Standard,* February 27, 1915.

———. "Aged Adirondack Guide Dead at Speculator." *Gloversville Morning Herald,* March 1, 1915.

———. "Stories Told of French Louie." *Gloversville Morning Herald,* March 4, 1915.

———. "Must Skidoo." *Lowville Journal and Republican,* Nov. 18, 1915.

———. "Last Call to Vacate." Lowville Journal and Republican, March 15, 1916.

———. "Salmon Lake Camps Burned by State Officials" *Lowville Journal and Republican,* Oct. 5, 1916.

———. "Week's End Chit-Chat." *Amsterdam Evening Recorder,* October 13, 1917.

———. "Is Unspoiled By Hand of Man." *Gloversville Morning Herald,* October 16, 1917.

———. "Elmiran In Charge." *Elmira Telegram,* November 7, 1920.

———. "Thief's Shot Hits Former Utica Woman." *Utica Observer-Dispatch,* August 12, 1930.

———. "Suspect Held in Connection with Shooting." *Utica Observer-Dispatch,* August 13, 1930.

———. "R. M. Gillespie, Right of Way Supervisor Dies." *The Upstater,* December 1935.

———. "Utican Urges Old Landmark Be Preserved." *Utica Observer-Dispatch,* September 26, 1938.

———. "Keep French Lewey's Fireplace." *Utica Observer-Dispatch,* September 27, 1938.

———. "For Honoring Woodsman." *New York Times,* October 16, 1938.

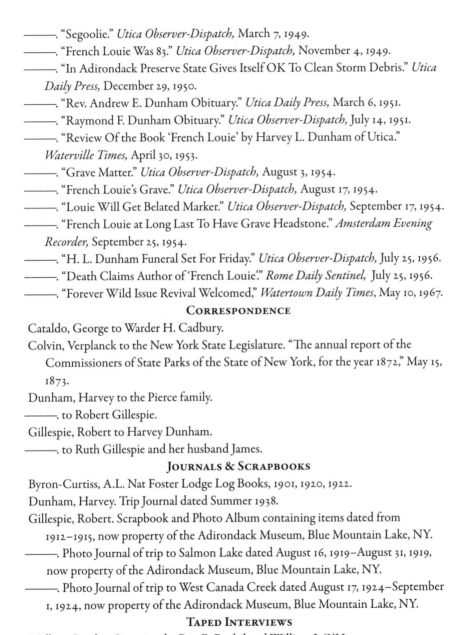

———. "Segoolie." *Utica Observer-Dispatch,* March 7, 1949.

———. "French Louie Was 83." *Utica Observer-Dispatch,* November 4, 1949.

———. "In Adirondack Preserve State Gives Itself OK To Clean Storm Debris." *Utica Daily Press,* December 29, 1950.

———. "Rev. Andrew E. Dunham Obituary." *Utica Daily Press,* March 6, 1951.

———. "Raymond F. Dunham Obituary." *Utica Observer-Dispatch,* July 14, 1951.

———. "Review Of the Book 'French Louie' by Harvey L. Dunham of Utica." *Waterville Times,* April 30, 1953.

———. "Grave Matter." *Utica Observer-Dispatch,* August 3, 1954.

———. "French Louie's Grave." *Utica Observer-Dispatch,* August 17, 1954.

———. "Louie Will Get Belated Marker." *Utica Observer-Dispatch,* September 17, 1954.

———. "French Louie at Long Last To Have Grave Headstone." *Amsterdam Evening Recorder,* September 25, 1954.

———. "H. L. Dunham Funeral Set For Friday." *Utica Observer-Dispatch,* July 25, 1956.

———. "Death Claims Author of 'French Louie.'" *Rome Daily Sentinel,* July 25, 1956.

———. "Forever Wild Issue Revival Welcomed," *Watertown Daily Times,* May 10, 1967.

CORRESPONDENCE

Cataldo, George to Warder H. Cadbury.

Colvin, Verplanck to the New York State Legislature. "The annual report of the Commissioners of State Parks of the State of New York, for the year 1872," May 15, 1873.

Dunham, Harvey to the Pierce family.

———. to Robert Gillespie.

Gillespie, Robert to Harvey Dunham.

———. to Ruth Gillespie and her husband James.

JOURNALS & SCRAPBOOKS

Byron-Curtiss, A.L. Nat Foster Lodge Log Books, 1901, 1920, 1922.

Dunham, Harvey. Trip Journal dated Summer 1938.

Gillespie, Robert. Scrapbook and Photo Album containing items dated from 1912–1915, now property of the Adirondack Museum, Blue Mountain Lake, NY.

———. Photo Journal of trip to Salmon Lake dated August 16, 1919–August 31, 1919, now property of the Adirondack Museum, Blue Mountain Lake, NY.

———. Photo Journal of trip to West Canada Creek dated August 17, 1924–September 1, 1924, now property of the Adirondack Museum, Blue Mountain Lake, NY.

TAPED INTERVIEWS

Malkin, Carolyn. Interview by Roy E. Reehil and William J. O'Hern.

Jones, Donna Pierce. Interview by Roy E. Reehil.

MISCELLANEOUS

Dunham, Harvey Leslie. Last Will and Testament.

State of New York. Adirondack Park State Land Master Plan.

Illustrations

Index

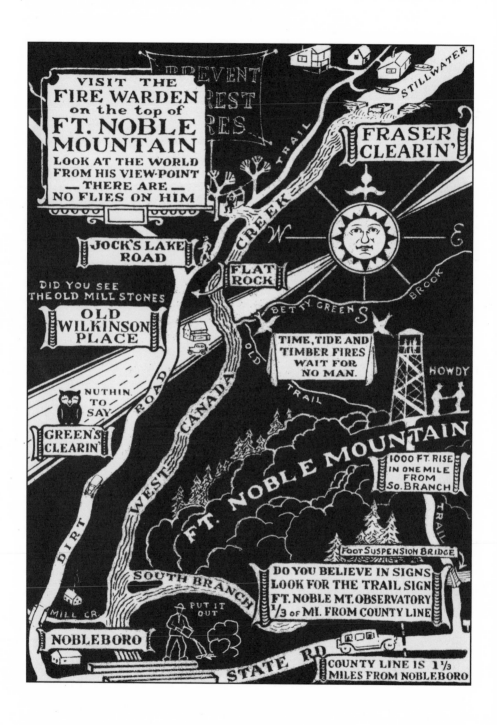